LILY CHIN'S

Crochet
*tips &
tricks

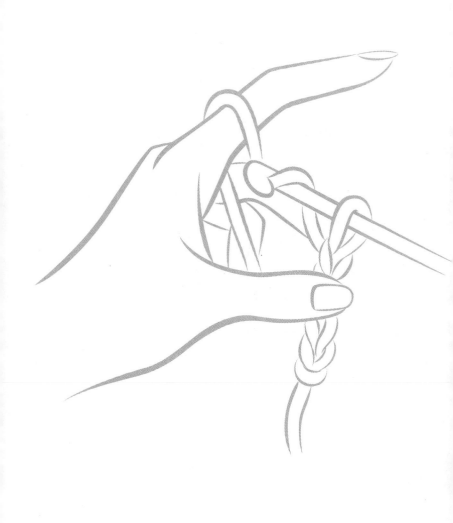

LILY CHIN'S
Crochet
*tips&
tricks

SHORTCUTS and **TECHNIQUES**
every crocheter should know

by Lily M. Chin

ILLUSTRATIONS BY LANA LE

POTTER
CRAFT
NEW YORK

Published in the United States by Potter Craft, an
imprint of the Crown Publishing Group, a division of
Random House, Inc., New York.

www.crownpublishing.com
wwww.pottercraft.com

POTTER CRAFT and colophon is a registered
trademark of Random House, Inc.

Library of Congress Cataloging-in-Publication Data

Lily Chin's Crochet Tips & Tricks:
Shortcuts and Techniques Every Crocheter
Should Know / by Lily M. Chin.

p. cm. Includes bibliographical references and index.

ISBN 978-0-307-46106-3

1. Crocheting. I. Title. II. Title: Crochet tips & tricks.

TT820.C484925 2009

746.43'4—dc22

2009021444

Printed in the United States

DESIGN BY CHALKLEY CALDERWOOD
ILLUSTRATIONS ON PAGES, 15, 22, 25, 33, 40, 41, 60, 70–77, 82–84, 88,
123, 125, 149, 151, 174, AND 184 BY FRANCES SOOHOO.
ALL OTHER ILLUSTRATIONS BY LANA LE

10 9 8 7 6 5 4 3 2 1

First Edition

This book is dedicated to the memories of my
recently deceased **mother** and **sister**.
They both nurtured my love of craft from an
early age and both left me way too soon.

Contents

4

As You Work

5

Finishing

Introduction

Having twice won the title of

"the world's fastest crocheter,"

I realized that the tips and tricks I've developed

over the years really do make crocheting go

both faster and easier.

I do a lot of teaching, my knitting class is hands-down

the most popular,

and I wanted to do the same for crochet. I've been

offering the crochet class for almost a decade and it

always sells out.

I envision this book as that very class brought to the
printed page—and my chance to share my techniques
with those who have voiced frustration at not
being able to attend a class.

Why You Need
This Book

THERE ARE TONS OF STANDARD TECHNIQUE BOOKS on the market right now. What you hold in your hands is not one of them. **It's a volume packed with all the little "a-ha" moments** I've had when faced with crochet problems and bugaboos. You may already be familiar with some of these solutions; others will be real eye-openers. **"Why didn't I think of that?"** is what I hear whenever I present these little tricks to my students—even those who have been crocheting for years. I may not be the first to employ or invent these techniques, but many of them have become more widespread, I'm sure, as a result of the classes that I have held almost every other month since 1997. Word gets around. I like to think that my "unventions"—that's the late knitting guru Elizabeth Zimmerman's term for coming up with something on your own, but knowing you can't possibly be the first to think of it—have **both enlightened experienced crocheters and helped beginners** start off on the right foot.

How to Use
This Book

MUCH AS I LOVE CROCHETING, there are certain aspects of
the process of which I'm not overly fond. (Can we say
"weave in the ends"?) **On these pages you'll find the
simple ways** I've devised to make the annoying parts
easier; hopefully they will make your crocheting life a lot
more enjoyable as well. The techniques are organized
chronologically and are presented in the order of
the crocheting process. They can be applied to any project,
so you can make use of them in your current work in
progress. You may not break my speed records, but
I guarantee your crocheting will go faster and be much
more fun. **Enjoy!**

1

In This Chapter

Hooks and Yarn

The tools and materials you work with can make all the difference between an enjoyable crochet experience and an exercise in frustration. **Choose good tools** and get yarn that's right for your project and enjoyable to work with. Take advantage of all that's available, and try out different hooks and yarns to see which work best for you.

The Hooks

• •

This basic crochet tool comes in many shapes
and sizes. There are lots of options—crochet
hooks can be shaped differently and are made
of many different materials.

Hook Types

What do you want to look for in a hook? A hook
is made up of a head, a throat, a shaft, a thumb
rest (or not), and a handle. There are two
distinct shapes to the head of a hook: round
and flat (also referred to as in-line). Boye is
one brand name for the former and Susan
Bates is a brand name for the latter. On either
type, the width of the shaft determines the size
of the stitches you will create.

Some crocheters say they like hooks with a
round head because the pointy top allows them
to get into the stitches more easily. Others
prefer hooks with a flat hook because it makes
pulling the yarn through the stitches smoother.
I encourage you to try both styles, in different
materials, to find what works best for you.
I favor the flat heads, but that's due to my own
movements in crocheting.

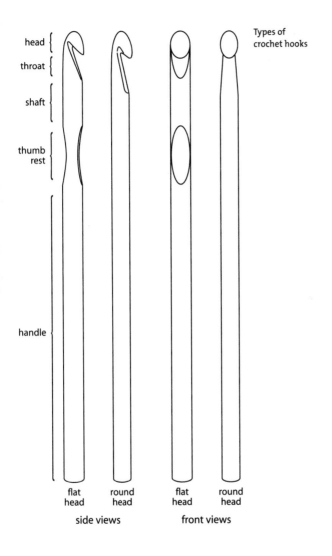

head

throat

shaft

thumb
rest

handle

Types of
crochet hooks

flat	round	flat	round
head	head	head	head
side views		front views	

Most hooks have a thumb rest or indent on the shaft that keeps the hook from rotating as you stitch. Some find this thumb rest useful and are annoyed by the lack of it; others do not. Again, try both types to decide whether this feature is important to you. I like it myself, but the choice of a hook is very personal.

Hook Materials

In the old days hooks were made from metal, bone, or wood (and occasionally more precious materials, such as ivory or tortoise shell). Today's hooks are made from many materials—everything from plastic, aluminum, and brass to exotic hardwoods, ecologically friendly bamboo, and glass. Some hooks are coated with nickel plating to speed stitching and some have an internal light source so they glow in the dark.

Hook Sizes

Hooks come in a large range of sizes. In the United States they are lettered and numbered. The higher the letter, the larger the hook; the number refers to the equivalent knitting needle size. In most of the rest of the world, however, hooks are measured in millimeters.

Crochet Hook Size

U.S. Size	Metric Size	UK/Canadian Size
B-1	2.25 mm	12
C-2	2.75 mm	11
D-3	3.25 mm	10
E-4	3.5 mm	9
F-5	3.75 mm	8
G-6	4 mm	7
7	4.5 mm	–
H-8	5 mm	6
I-9	5.5 mm	5
J-10	6 mm	4
K-10½	6.5 mm	2
L-11	8 mm	–
M-13	9 mm	–
N-15	10 mm	–
P-16	11.5 mm	–
Q	16 mm	–
S	19 mm	–

To confuse things even further, some hooks used in the UK go by an older numbering system in which the larger the number, the smaller the hook. The previous table lists the sizes and their equivalents.

Steel Crochet Hook Size

U.S. Size	Metric Size	UK/Canadian Size
14	.75mm	–
13	.85mm	7
12	1.0mm	6 $\frac{1}{2}$
11	1.1mm	6
10	1.3mm	5 $\frac{1}{2}$
9	1.4mm	5
8	1.5mm	4 $\frac{1}{2}$
7	1.65mm	4
6	1.8mm	3 $\frac{1}{2}$
5	1.9mm	3
4	2.0mm	2 $\frac{1}{2}$
3	2.1mm	2
2	2.25mm	1 $\frac{1}{2}$
1	2.75mm	1
0	3.25mm	0
00	3.5mm	–

STEEL HOOKS. Those tiny hooks usually used with crochet thread for lacemaking and filet crochet and other thread work, use yet another sizing system. Numbering systems vary for these hooks so you'll come across several different conversion charts for them. One such chart is at the left.

● **TIP** A MYSTERY HOOK

Fortunately, most hooks are marked with their size, usually on the thumb rest or at the bottom of the handle. But if you find a hook with no indication of its size, you might be tempted to stick it through a device called a gauge check made of plastic or metal with holes in it. If the head is big, as it is with the round head, the head will not go through the hole of the proper size. For these hooks, try comparing the size of the shaft of the mystery hook to an existing hook whose size is labeled. Roll them together between your fingers and compare them.

Yarns

· ·

Today's yarn market offers a dizzying array of choices in color, fiber, texture, and weight. The type of project you're making helps dictate the type of yarn you choose. Baby yarn is for baby items, worsted weight yarn for afghans. I like soft, drapey yarns for camisoles and thicker yarns for jackets and coats. Pure wool, which is naturally flame-retardant, is great for potholders and oven mitts. Some yarns are even treated to make them antibacterial, great if you're making items for the little ones; others contain aloe to soften the hands as you work.

Yarn Fibers

Yarns are now made up of many different materials, often referred to as content. There is the traditional wool and cotton (natural fibers) and acrylic (man-made) or the more exotic fibers of the alpaca, angora rabbit, angora goat (mohair), the cashmere goat, and even New Zealand possum and the occasional handspun dog hair! Qiviut, which comes from the down of the Arctic musk ox, is beautiful, but quite rare and expensive. Vicuña, an even more uncommon and expensive yarn from a relative of the South American alpaca or llama, is also gaining popularity. In my stash, I have such rarities as yarn from fox, chinchilla, mink, yak, and buffalo.

Blending of different fibers can impart the
best of all worlds. A bit of acrylic can make
an inelastic cotton light and stretchy or make
wool machine washable and/or dryable. The
addition of wool to a luxury fiber like cashmere
or alpaca can change the properties of the
fiber and make it more affordable.

Yarn Construction

Type	Description
Bouclé	From French word meaning "curl." Loopy. Often hard to see stitches.
Chenille	Fuzzy, plush. Beware of tendency to worm (or loop out), and to bias and shed.
Eyelash	Hairy, fuzzy. Often hard to see stitches.
Microfiber	Very fine thicknesses achieved mostly with synthetic fibers.
Ribbon	Flat tape. Can be crocheted or woven.
Slubs, Nubby, Thick and Thin	Uneven thickness of yarn throughout. Sometimes lumps or bumps appear after thin areas.

Yarn Texture

Fuzzy, smooth, nubby, or with tufts, yarn comes in all sorts of textures. Classic spinning and plying methods create a smooth yarn, but there are plenty of "novelty" yarns. Bouclé has bubbly loops, brushed yarn is hairy, tape looks like ribbon. Combine construction with content and you get yarns such as a cashmere ribbon, a mohair bouclé, a brushed acrylic, and more.

flat tape or ribbon

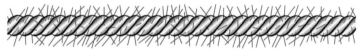

fuzzy or hairy

bouclé

● **TIP** MORE (FUZZ) THAN MEETS THE EYE
Certain yarns may seem small on the skein, but will work up to a larger stitch (and gauge) than you would expect. Fuzzy fibers, such as mohair, or yarn that takes up airspace, such as bouclé, can be deceiving.

Yarn Thickness

U.S mills have traditionally spun certain standard thicknesses for the commercial hand-knitting and crochet markets. These weights are known as fingering, sport, worsted, and bulky. Traditionally, finer yarns are used for socks, underwear, and baby items. Since there are more stitches required to complete them, these items, though small, may take the same amount of time as a larger item (such as an adult sweater) in a medium- or heavyweight yarn. The advantage of using finer-weight yarns is that the fabric produced is thinner and drapes nicely. Bulkier yarns are usually used for jackets and outerwear. Though the resulting fabric is generally chunkier and does not drape as well, projects made with these yarns are, by and large, quicker to finish.

For more on how thick or thin yarns are, I refer you to the website of the Craft Yarn Council of America and its yarn standards (http://yarnstandards.com/weight.html). Not only does this site contain useful charts of needle sizes and yarn weights, it gives you great information on standard abbreviations, yarn label information for care of the project, size and garment measurements, and other guidelines.

A good place to start with yarn weight is to look at the information on the yarn label. There is usually a recommended gauge size, such as 4 stitches per inch (2.5 cm) or 6 stitches per inch (2.5 cm) as well as a suggested needle size. Remember that these are just recommendations and suggestions. Feel free to use the needle size that will get the recommended gauge. Conversely, if you feel the fabric of your swatch is just fine on the needles that you've chosen, but those are different than those suggested on the label, feel free to deviate.

Yarn thickness

Yarn Content

Type	Origin	Characteristics/Comments
Wool	**Sheep** (including Merino, Shetland, Icelandic)	Versatile, warm, and very elastic. Feel and appearance can vary with breed.
Silk	**Silkworm** (a cocoon secretion)	Slick and sleek. Both warm and cool with no elasticity.
Alpaca	**Alpaca** (from South America)	Warm with medium elasticity.
Mohair	**Angora goat**	Hairy or fuzzy. Warm with limited elasticity.
Angora	**Angora rabbit**	Very hairy. Very warm with limited elasticity.
Camel Hair	**Camel**	Warm with medium elasticity.
Llama	**Llama** (cousin to the alpaca; originally from South America)	Warm with medium elasticity.
Cashmere	**Goat**	Very warm and luxurious. Medium elasticity.
Yak	**Yak**	Very rare. Warm and limited elasticity.
Qiviut	**Arctic musk ox**	Similar to cashmere but warmer.
Guanaco	**Guanaco** (a threatened relative of the llama from South America)	Very rare and expensive. Warm with limited elasticity.
Vicuña	**Vicuña** (an endangered relative of the llama from South America)	Very rare and expensive. Warm with limited elasticity.

Type	Origin	Characteristics/Comments
Cotton	Cotton plant	Cool. Can be left matte in its natural state or made shiny through mercerization. No elasticity.
Linen	Flax plant	Stiff, but softens upon washing. Cool with no elasticity.
Rayon/Tencel	Reconstituted tree pulp	Cool and slinky with no elasticity.
Bamboo	Reconstituted bamboo pulp	Smooth and cool with no elasticity.
Ramie	Reconstituted pulp of ramie plant	Combines the properties of cotton and linen. Cool with no elasticity.
Hemp	Hemp plant	Linenlike. No elasticity.
Soy	Soybean by-product	Cool. No elasticity.
Banana Fiber/Corn	Reconstituted fiber (from fruit tree bark or corn plant)	Cool with no elasticity.
Milk Protein	Milk casein (milk protein)	Cool with no elasticity.
Chitin	Reconstituted shrimp and crab shells	Cool with no elasticity.
Metallics/Metals	Metals	Slinky or scratchy, depending on the metal used and construction method. Shiny and cool, some can be sculpted.

European and Australian Standards

Imported yarn often uses different weight standards. In the United Kingdom and throughout most of Europe, you will get names such as four-ply, double-knitting (or DK), Aran, and chunky. To confound things even further, Australia classifies their thicknesses as four-ply, six-ply, eight-ply, and so on, even though there may not be that many strands or plies in that yarn. See the chart below for the Australian yarn equivalents. As you can see, even if the names are different, the recommended gauge is a great

Australian Yarn

Australian Yarn	Gauge per 10 cm (4 inches)	Needle Size	U.S. Weight	CYCA Category
3-ply	32 stitches/40 rows	3.25mm (U.S. 3)	Fingering	0 Lace
4-ply	28 stitches/36 rows	3.25mm (U.S. 3)	Sock, fingering, baby	1 Superfine
5-ply	26 stitches	3.75mm (U.S. 5)	Sport, baby	2 Fine
8-ply	22 stitches	4mm (U.S. 6)	DK	3 Light
10-ply	20 stitches	4.5mm (U.S. 7)	Light worsted	3 Light
12-ply	17–18 stitches	5–5.5mm (U.S. 8–9)	Worsted	4 Medium
14-ply	14–15 stitches	6–6.5mm (U.S. 10–10.5)	Chunky	5 Bulky

clue to the yarn weights. Again, refer to the standard yarn weights chart from the Craft Yarn Council for help in sorting out yarn thicknesses.

● **TIP** WRAPS PER INCH

Another method of classifying yarn weights is a system used primarily by weavers. Wrap a yarn around a pencil or ruler and count how many wraps there are in an inch. The heavier the yarn, the fewer wraps; the thinner the yarn, the more wraps. Here is a table of wraps per inch for U.S. yarn weights.

Wraps

Yarn (U.S.)	Wraps Per Inch
Fingering	17–18 wpi
Sport	15–16 wpi
DK	14 wpi
Worsted	12–13 wpi
Aran	10–11 wpi
Bulky	8–9 wpi
Super Bulky	6–7 wpi

Unraveling the Secrets of Cone Yarn

The industrial-type yarns that are usually found on cones use a mysterious series of numbers such as 5/2 or 2/28. These counts indicate thickness of the yarn and the number of plies. It is an international standard used by the manufacturing industry. Yarns used for weaving and for machine knitting are more commonly found in these put-ups than those intended for hand-knitting or crocheting. There are actually a few different systems, but the worsted system for wool and acrylic fibers is one of the most typical.

The Worsted System

In this system the first number indicates the number of plies. So, for example, 1/5.5 means the yarn is a single-ply or has only one strand in the yarn. The second number is based on *length per fixed weight*, which in this case is one pound (454g). The number of yards per pound will vary, but for whatever reason, it's measured by how many 560-yard (512m) hanks there are in this pound.

The higher the number, the thinner the yarn. For example, it takes a whopping 2,000 yards (1829m) of a sport weight yarn to make a pound, but only 800 yards (732m) of a worsted weight. In a single-ply, the sport weight would be 1/3.5 (it takes three-and-a-half 560-yard hanks to get 2,000 yards in a pound) and the worsted would be a 1/1.4 (it takes one and four-tenths 560-yard hanks to get 800 yards in a pound).

So let's say it takes five-and-a-half hanks of 560 yards each to weigh this pound and the yarn is a single-ply. That would be 1/5.5. Here's the math you'd use to figure out the yarn weight: 5.5 times 560 equals 3,080 (2,816m) yards per pound. A pound is equal to 454 grams, and 3,080 yards divided by 454 equals 6.78 yards (6.2m) per gram. This means a 50-gram ball has 339 yards, which would be similar to a British four-ply weight (between sport and fingering weight).

A 2/28 means there are two plies and that each of the plies is so thin that it took twenty-eight hanks at 560 yards each to achieve this pound—actually 15,680 yards (14,338m) total.

The Cotton System

Cotton is similar to the worsted system, but the numbers are inverted and use hanks of 840 yards instead of 560 yards. Thus, a 5/2 yarn has two plies and each one requires five hanks of 840 yards (768m) to equal a pound.

The Denier System

The denier system is used for continuous-filament silk spinning. So when nylon (or artificial silk) came onto the scene, it was also measured in a denier count, which is a measurement of the weight per fixed length. It is the opposite of the worsted system. Instead of the weight being fixed, the yardage is fixed. The fixed unit length is 9,000 meters (9,843 yards). So you want to know how much 9,000 meters of any given yarn weighs. Obviously, 9,000 meters of a thick yarn would weigh way more than 9,000 meters of a thin one.

Unlike the worsted system—where the higher the number, the finer the yarn—here, it's the lower the number the finer the yarn. So a filament of 2 denier is twice as thick as a filament of only 1 denier. By the way, 1 denier means this yarn weighs a mere 1 gram per 9,000 meters. Anything thinner than this is classified as a microfiber, which has a general thickness of one-sixtieth of a human hair!

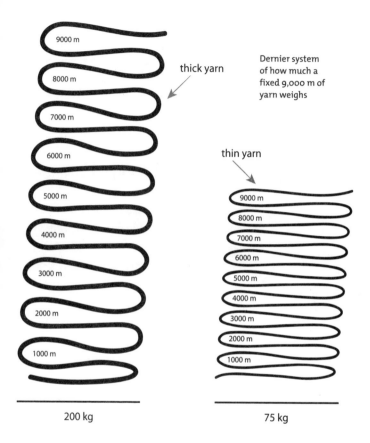

9000 m

8000 m

thick yarn

7000 m

Dernier system
of how much a
fixed 9,000 m of
yarn weighs

6000 m

thin yarn

5000 m

4000 m

9000 m

3000 m

8000 m

7000 m

2000 m

6000 m

5000 m

1000 m

4000 m

3000 m

2000 m

1000 m

200 kg

75 kg

The Tex System

The tex system was introduced as a universal system to replace all existing systems, but it has not been widely accepted. It is measured by the number of grams per 1 kilometer or 1,000 meters of yarn, not dissimilar to the denier system. In this system, a 50-gram ball of our DK or light-worsted crocheting yarn typically measures about 100 meters (109 yards). That means 1,000 meters would weigh 500 grams (1.1 pounds) so the yarn is 500 tex. The number of plies and the direction in which the plies are twisted together are also included in the designation. For example, on a label that reads "R 500 Tex / 4 S," *R* means resulting count or total count, and *4 S* means there are four plies twisted in a counterclockwise direction or S-twist (as opposed to a clockwise or Z-twist). However, each one of the four plies has a 125 tex since the four combined make up 500 tex (or R).

To summarize, here are the basics of the most common systems.

- **Bradford Worsted System:** The number of 560-yard (512m) hanks that weigh

1 pound (454g).

- **English Woolen System:** The number of 256-yard (243m) hanks that will weigh 1 pound (454g).

- **English Cotton System:** The number of 840-yard (768m) hanks that will weigh 1 pound (454g).

- **Continental Metric System:** The number of 1,000-meter or kilometer (1,094-yard) hanks that will weigh 1,000 grams or kilogram (35 ounces).

- **Denier System:** The weight in grams of 9,000 meters (9,843 yards).

- **Tex System:** The weight in grams of 1,000 meters (1,094 yards).

If all this seems confusing, just remember that worsted-weight yarn is 1,000 yards (917m) per pound, sport weight yarn is about 1,500–1,800 yards (1,375–1,651m) per pound, and fingering weight is around 2,000 yards (1,829m) per pound.

On the other hand, if this subject fascinates you, do an online search for "yarn numbering system" to learn more.

● **TIP** MATCHING HOOKS TO YARNS

The key to crochet success lies in knowing how to match the different hook types to yarn type. Not only do you want to use the proper hook size with the proper weight of yarn, you'll also see that the type of hook can make crocheting with a particular type of yarn easier and more pleasant. For a slippery yarn, such as a mercerized cotton or a slinky rayon, use a grabby hook type, such as bamboo, wood, or even some plastic varieties. When the yarn is grabby, such as a matte chenille, try a slick nickel-plated hook. A luxury yarn like angora might call for an equally high-end hook like ebony, just for the sheer decadence of it!

If you find yourself struggling with your project, a change of tools may make things easier. Another type of hook, even in the same size, can alter your gauge. Experiment with a few different ones. If you find that you can't seem to get gauge, try birch instead of aluminum or plastic instead of bamboo. Hooks can also induce "moods" into your piece. Metal, cold to the touch, can cause some crocheters to tense up. Wood, which is warmer to the touch, can relax other crocheters. These factors can also affect your gauge.

British Stitch Names

● ●

The basic crochet stitches have different
names, depending on whether you are reading
American or British directions. The U.S. single
crochet is the equivalent of the UK double
crochet, and U.S. double crochet stitch is
referred to as a treble crochet in the UK. The
following chart will help you follow a pattern
from England:

British Stitch Names

U.S. Term	UK Term
chain	chain
slip stitch	slip stitch or tight stitch
single crochet	double crochet
half double crochet	half treble crochet
double crochet	treble crochet
treble crochet	double treble crochet
double treble crochet	triple treble crochet

In This Chapter

The Basics

This book addresses crocheting right-handed. I often encourage left-handed beginners to try to crochet right-handed simply because it will make following pattern instructions **a lot easier** later. If you find you can't quite grasp this, just put the book up to a mirror and view the illustrations that way.

Holding the Hook

There are two basic ways to hold a crochet hook: the knife hold and the pencil hold. Crocheters are very opinionated about which is the proper way to hold the hook, but, trust me, it is truly a matter of personal preference. Use the one that works best for you.

In Victorian times, the pencil hold was preferred because it appeared more lady-like and dainty. I personally prefer the knife hold. I feel I have better control that way, and I find it easier on my hand and wrist because the moves are not contorted for me. Try both ways to see which one you like better.

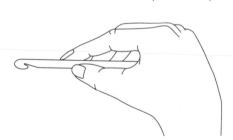

Pencil hold

Knife hold

Holding the Yarn

Some crocheters like to hold the yarn with
the index finger up; others prefer to hold the
index finger down. Either way, most wind
the yarn around the pinky finger of the left
hand (for right-handers), then up and over
the index finger. I hold my finger up rather
high because it allows me to see the yarn and
hook better, and gives me greater tension.

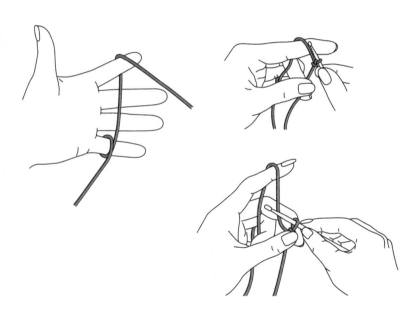

● **TIP** KEEPING THE HOOK SMOOTH

Unless you are using the more expensive nickel-plated styles, which are very slick, the hook may drag from time to time. You can compensate for this by revitalizing and smoothing the surface of your hook.

I take a bit of hand cream or lotion to coat the tips of my hooks, then tissue it off. This leaves a nice, slick residue. Every month, I wash the hooks and reapply the lotion. This little trick gives me an edge in speed competitions and has helped me win my "fastest crocheter" titles.

Some crocheters use wax paper to gloss over the hook; others suggest rubbing the hook through the hair and scalp to pick up natural oils. I find the cream method to be longer lasting than the hair treatment, and more readily available than the wax paper method. (I always have some kind of cream or lotion around but I don't necessarily have access to wax paper.) In a pinch, when traveling, I've even used liquid soap from public restrooms!

If your hooks develop nicks or burrs, use an emery board or fine sandpaper to smooth them down, and then apply the cream or lotion. The hook will be as good as new. I do this for almost all types of hooks from wood to aluminum to plastic.

Crochet Basics

· ·

Crochet is not as old as knitting, and its origins are still a bit of a mystery. Some surmise that the craft evolved in Arabia, South America, or China; it became popular in Europe during the 1800s. It is fascinating to me—as it must have been to those early crocheters—how you can take a piece of string and manipulate loops to create a piece of fabric or sculpture. The structure of crocheting is not difficult to figure out. If you study the way the loops are picked up and then finished off, one at a time, you will have a better understanding of the craft. Once you see what crochet is composed of, you will see its many possibilities.

The Foundation Chain

The foundation chain is one of the very basics of crochet. Appropriately named, it lays down a foundation. Each chain is considered a stitch: The more chain stitches there are, the wider the piece. Other stitches are worked one at a time across the chain, creating what is called a row. More rows of stitches are worked over these stitches to create the vertical height of the piece.

A slip knot

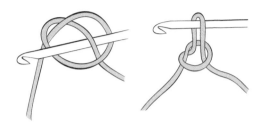

To begin a chain (commonly abbreviated in instructions as ch) you start with a slip knot. What's a slip knot? It's a loop of yarn that can be easily untied. Take your yarn, make a loop as shown, and insert your hook. If you take your hook out of the loop and pull on the yarn end, the knot will come undone. You don't want the knot to pull out when you crochet. It should stay on the hook.

To begin the chain: With the slip knot on the hook (not too loose or too tight), wrap the yarn around the hook and pull the yarn through the slip knot. You have made one chain.

Make the next chain by wrapping the yarn around the hook and pulling it through the loop on the hook. Continue this way for each subsequent chain stitch. As you work, you'll see that it's called a chain because it does, indeed, look like one. You will make as many chains as called for in the directions.

Making a chain

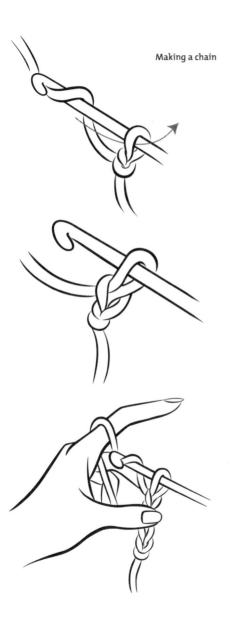

A chain

Anatomy of a Chain

When working into the chain, the front will usually be facing you. The back of the chain has a nub on it that looks like a purl stitch in knitting. The pattern instructions will tell you to work in the second, third, or fourth chain from the hook. The loop on the hook is not counted as a stitch, nor is the initial slip knot. If you spread the chain apart, you will see that the chain comprises three strands, with the one in the middle pushed to the back. When you work into the chain, the hook usually goes under the top two strands.

Some patterns will tell you to work into the top loop only. This creates more of a gap, however, because the stitch above the chain pulls on just one strand of yarn.

The front of a chain

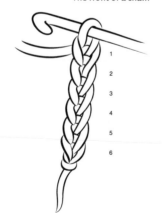

1
2
3
4
5
6

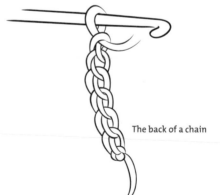

The back of a chain

The Single Crochet Stitch

The single crochet (abbreviated as sc) is a short stitch. To make a single crochet, insert the hook into the second chain from the hook, wrap the yarn around the hook, and pull up a loop. There are now two loops on the hook. Wrap the yarn around the hook again, and pull the yarn through both the loops on the hook. Repeat these steps in each chain to complete a row.

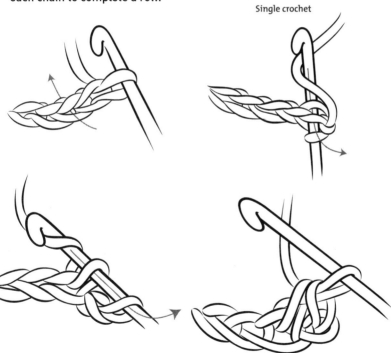

Single crochet

Turning Chains

When you are ready to work your next row, your work needs to be at the right height to match the stitches you are making. To do this, you will make what is called a turning chain. The pattern usually tells you how many chains to make, whether to make them at the end of the row or the beginning of the next row, and whether or not the turning chain counts as one stitch.

This shows the number of chains you need for each stitch.

THE NEXT ROW. At the end of each row, you will turn the work. If you are working in single crochet, you will chain one to achieve about the height of the single crochet stitch, then work into each single crochet. Where do you insert your hook? Look for the V's across the tops of the stitches. Insert the hook underneath both "legs" of each V. Sometimes a pattern will tell you to work into only one of these legs, either the front one or the back one. Do not work into the chain-1 at the beginning of the previous row (which is now at the end of the row you're working across).

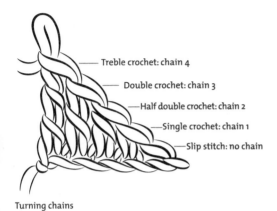

Treble crochet: chain 4

Double crochet: chain 3

Half double crochet: chain 2

Single crochet: chain 1

Slip stitch: no chain

Turning chains

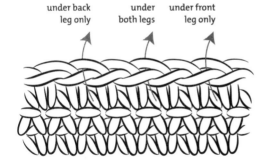

under back
leg only

under
both legs

under front
leg only

Working into
rows of single
crochet

The Half Double Crochet Stitch

Next in height is the half double crochet stitch (or hdc). To create the extra height, wrap the yarn around the hook first, and then insert the hook into the third chain from the hook. Wrap the yarn around the hook again and pull a loop through the chain. There are now three loops on the hook. Wrap the yarn around the hook again and pull through all three loops on the hook. Repeat these steps in each subsequent chain to complete the row.

On subsequent rows, turn the work, chain two to achieve about the height of the half double crochet stitch, then skip the first half double crochet stitch. You skip the first stitch because the chain-2 at the beginning of the row has substituted for the half double crochet stitch that would normally go into the first stitch. Work into each half double crochet after this, inserting the hook under both legs of each V across (unless the pattern directions tell you otherwise). Do not forget to work into the top chain of the chain-2 at the beginning of the previous row (which is now at the end of the row you're working across).

Half double crochet

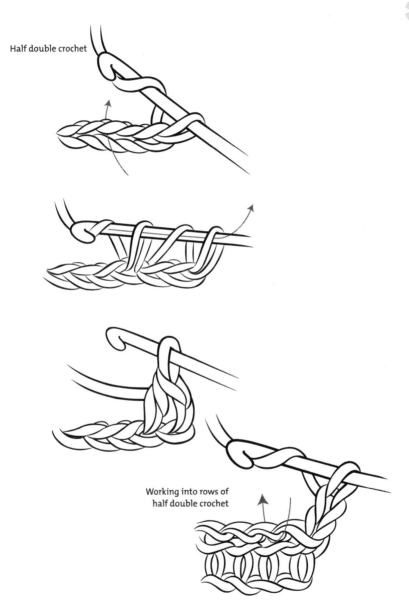

Working into rows of
half double crochet

The Double Crochet Stitch

Even higher is the double crochet stitch (or dc). To make a double crochet stitch, wrap the yarn around the hook first, and then insert the hook into the fourth chain from hook. Wrap the yarn around the hook again and pull up a loop through the chain.

There are now three loops on the hook. Wrap the yarn around the hook and pull through the first two the loops on the hook. Wrap the yarn around the hook once more and pull through the remaining two loops on the hook. Repeat this in each subsequent chain to complete a row.

On subsequent rows, turn the work. Chain 3 to achieve about the height of the double crochet stitch, then skip the first double crochet. This is because the chain-3 at the beginning of the row has substituted for the double crochet stitch that would normally go into the first double crochet. Work into each double crochet after this, inserting the hook under both legs of each V across (unless the pattern directions tell you otherwise). Do not forget to work into the top chain of the chain-3 at the beginning of the previous row (now at the end of the row you're working across).

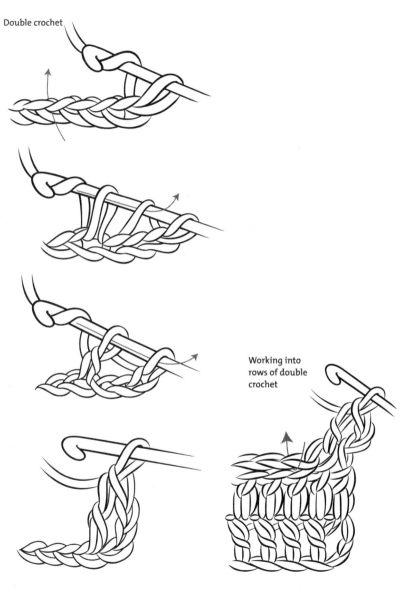

Double crochet

Working into rows of double crochet

The Treble Crochet Stitch

The treble crochet stitch, sometimes called triple crochet (and abbreviated as tr), is the tallest of the basic stitches. To make a treble crochet, wrap the yarn around the hook twice, then insert the hook into the fifth chain from the hook, and pull a loop through the chain. There are now four loops on the hook. Wrap the yarn around the hook and pull it through only two loops on the hook. Wrap the yarn around the hook and pull it through the next two loops on the hook. Wrap the yarn around the hook once more and pull through the remaining two loops on the hook. Repeat this in each subsequent chain to complete a row.

On subsequent rows, turn the work. Chain 4 to achieve about the height of the treble crochet, then skip the first treble crochet. This is because the chain-4 at the beginning of the row has substituted for the treble crochet stitch that would normally go into the first stitch. Work into each treble crochet after this, inserting the hook underneath both legs of each V across (unless pattern directions tell you otherwise). Do not forget to work into the top chain of the chain-4 at the beginning of the previous row (now at the end of the row you're working across).

Treble crochet

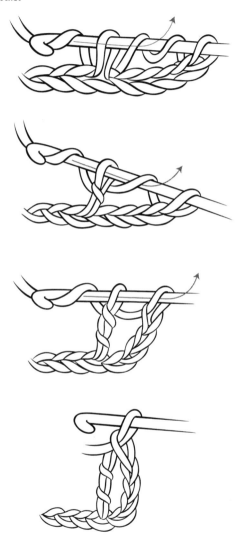

The Slip Stitch

Unlike the previous stitches, the slip stitch (or sl st) is not used to create an all-over crocheted fabric. (Doing so would be rather tedious and slow going as the stitch is short and adds virtually no height.) Instead it is used at the beginning of rows where you want to skip over those first few stitches—in the bottom of an armhole, for example. The slip stitch is also used to join rows of circular pieces (otherwise known as rounds), and to seam pieces together.

To work a slip stitch, insert the hook into a chain or other stitch, wrap the yarn around the hook and then draw the yarn through both the stitch and the loop already on the hook.

Slip stitch

Mixing Stitches to Create Patterns

By combining these basic stitches, you can create an infinite number of patterns and textures. Lace, for instance, involves making a chain stitch and then skipping over several subsequent stitches to create holes or open spaces. Rows of short stitches, such as single crochet, can alternate with rows of long stitches, such as double crochet. More than one stitch can be worked into another stitch, either to increase the number of stitches to make the piece wider or to create a fanning-out pattern, such as the shell stitch. I strongly recommend investing in a stitch dictionary to check out the many lovely and intriguing patterns.

3

In This Chapter

Getting Started

Most crocheters are chomping at the bit to begin their project. Take a deep breath and always start with a **gauge swatch.** (Think of it as predicting the future, not as a chore.) Learn how to find the center of a yarn ball **more easily,** and create a better beginning foundation chain. Your crochet will be better for it.

Making a Swatch

One of the very first things you make before you begin a project is the gauge swatch. Getting the correct gauge when crocheting a garment is crucial if you want the garment to fit. (It's not so crucial for items such as scarves or afghans that don't have to be an exact sizes.) If you're making a garment and refuse to swatch, all I can say is that you get what you deserve!

What is Gauge?

And why is getting the gauge important? Gauge is the number of stitches and the number of rows it takes to get a certain measurement. That measurement is usually taken over a 4-inch (10cm) square, though many instructions list gauge in terms of one inch, such as "4 stitches per inch" or

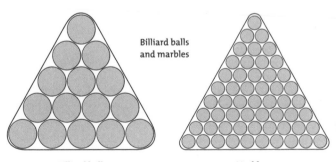

Billiard balls and marbles

Billiard balls

Marbles

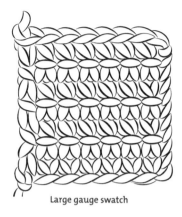

Large gauge swatch

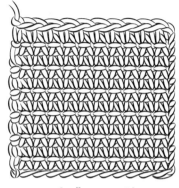

Small gauge swatch

"5 rows per inch." If the size measurement of your stitches and your rows do not match that of the pattern, the piece you crochet will not end up the intended size.

If you are familiar with the game of billiards or pool, you know that the 15 billiard balls fit into the triangular-shaped rack. What if you filled the rack with marbles rather than those fat billiard balls? How many marbles will fit into that same triangular rack? A whole lot more.

Now instead of a triangular rack, imagine a square one that is 4 inches by 4 inches (10cm x 10cm). The number of stitches that fit into that square rack is the gauge. Heavy and bulky yarns are your billiard balls. The stitches are so big that you can only fit a small amount (say, twelve) in there. The thinner and finer yarns are the marbles. The stitches are smaller so you can fit a large amount, perhaps as many as twenty-four, in the square.

If your gauge is larger or looser than called for (fewer stitches and rows in a 4-inch [10cm] swatch), the piece will be too big. Conversely, if your gauge is smaller or tighter than that called for (more stitches and rows in a 4-inch [10cm] swatch), the finished piece will be too small.

Exactly how big should your swatch be? Almost all measurements are specified for a 4-inch (10cm) square. Since the edges do not lie flat, you want to make a swatch bigger than that. I like 6-inch (15cm) square so I can make a 1-inch (2.5cm) border all around. If the gauge is given for a repeat of a stitch pattern, work the border in either plain stitches on either side or work more of the pattern on each side. If the repeat is very large, work plain stitches.

TIP MARKING YOUR SWATCH

After making a gauge swatch, you may not always begin the project immediately. You may
lose the hook or use it for some other project.
You may have gotten gauge the first time,
but it does you little good if you've forgotten
the size of the hook you used to get there.

To jog your memory, I suggest working
picot stitches across the top of the swatch
as a reminder of the hook size you used.
Make the same number of picot stitches as
the hook size: One stitch for size A, two
for size B, three for size C, and so on. So if
you see seven picots on the swatch, you
know it was done on a size G hook.

To work a picot, slip stitch, chain 3, slip
stitch again, all in the same stitch. Add
a single crochet stitch between each picot
so the picots will lie flat.

A swatch
marked
with picots
across the top

Washing and Blocking the Swatch

Do you think you'll ever launder your projects? Well, most of us plan to wash our crocheted items at some point. The golden rule of crocheting is "Do unto the swatch what you will do to the project." How else can you know if the black and white stripes will become a gray blur. Or if that silk yarn will grow or that cotton shrink. You don't want any surprises in the finished garment. The swatch will tell all. Measure the swatch and take note of its condition before and the after washing to see if there are any changes. Some crocheters like to wet block but I prefer steam blocking (page 170).

Would you buy a diamond ring without having it appraised first? Think of swatch-making as appraising your yarn. I frequently buy just one skein of a yarn before investing in all the yarn needed for the entire project. Will that cashmere pill? Will that wool hold up under some wear and tear? I pin the swatch to the inside of my garments and wear it around or stuff it inside my purse. I call this the torture test. If it still looks good and not too worn, I will then buy all the yarn I need. It's better to know sooner, rather than later, that my time and effort will be rewarded.

Many yarns are labeled "dry clean only." Manufacturers do this to minimize their liability. I know for a fact that many of these yarns can indeed be hand-washed. How can I tell? You guessed it; I wash the swatch. You'll find that you can save yourself some costly dry-cleaning bills and be more environmentally friendly at the same time.

● **TIP** CONDITIONING YOUR WOOL YARN

If your wool is rough and scratchy, pour a little hair conditioner or creme rinse into the wash. This will soften the fabric considerably. After all, what are woolens but animal hair, and animal hair will respond to conditioner just as your hair does.

Measuring the Swatch

Use a ruler or other straightedge (not a flexible tape measure) to measure the stitches in your swatch in several places. Gauge can vary over the width of the swatch (you may stitch tightly when you are stressed, more loosely if you're relaxed) so play it safe by taking a measurement in a few spots and averaging them out. If the measurements differ significantly from one spot to the next, crochet the swatch again.

TIP READING THE GAUGE

If you have difficulty distinguishing individual stitches in the swatch, try using a contrasting yarn. You'll need two 8-inch (20.5cm) strands of a smooth yarn of similar weight in a contrasting color. Let's say the gauge is sixteen single crochet equals 4 inches (10cm). If you're making a 6-inch (15cm) square, there should be twenty-four single crochet with four stitches on either side of the center sixteen. After completing the first row, work the first four stitches, place the contrasting yarn to the left of the last stitch and work the next sixteen stitches,

Swatch with contrasting yarn marking off the stitches

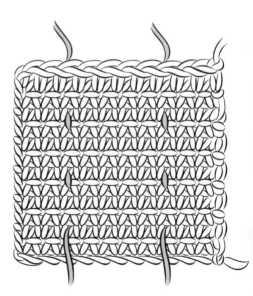

place the other contrasting yarn to the left of the last stitch, then work the last four stitches. Continue this way, carrying the contrasting yarn up between the stitches. When the swatch is complete, these contrasting yarn strands will look like basting threads, and you will be able to measure the distance between them to see how many inches the sixteen stitches equals.

If your yarn is dark or highly textured, here is a tip to make it easier to find the gauge. Let's say the gauge is sixteen single crochet stitches and twenty single crochet rows equals 4 inches (10cm). Using a contrasting

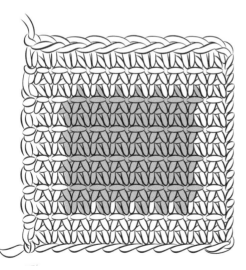

Color-block swatch

color yarn of the same weight, begin with the chain and a row or two of the contrasting color. If you're making a 6-inch (15cm) swatch, there should be twenty-four single crochet. Now using the intarsia method (page 127) with separate bobbins for each yarn color, on the next row, work the first four stitches in the contrasting color, switch to the project color for the middle sixteen stitches, then switch back to the contrast color for the last four stitches. Work this way for exactly twenty rows, then end with a row or two of the contrasting color. You will have a square block of your color and be able to clearly mark sixteen single crochet and twenty single crochet rows.

● **TIP** SEEING THE GAUGE

If you are working with a novelty yarn that is heavily textured, lumpy, fuzzy, or bumpy, it can be difficult to see the stitches clearly enough to read the gauge. That's when you have to see the light. Tape the swatch to a window on a sunny day. The light will stream through the swatch, and you'll be able to count the stitches for the gauge.

Even if you're not concerned about gauge (on an afghan, for example), crocheting with novelty yarns can be problematic. The stitches in black mohair or navy eyelash can be difficult to see and you'll have trouble figuring out exactly where to insert the hook. Use light again, this time by placing a lamp on the floor. The backlighting should make it easier to see the stitches. Some crocheters place a light-colored towel or cloth on their laps for a similar effect.

I have a doctor friend who tapes her swatches to an X-ray viewing machine when she's working the graveyard shift. What a funny sight that must be.

The Hung Gauge

Most crocheters measure their swatches on a flat surface. That's fine for an afghan, but if the project is a garment you will now know how big this garment will be if you were to wear it while lying down in bed! Should you decide to stand up or even sit up, guess what? Think about that force in nature that Sir Isaac Newton discovered in the mid-1600s. Gravity will take its toll (so have proper change). You can mimic the effects of gravity on the crocheted fabric by hanging up the swatch. I use masking tape to secure my swatches to the wall, but straight pins along a towel hanging on the rack or push-pins on a corkboard will work equally well. This creates a more accurate picture of what the fabric will measure once it grows up, or in this case, grows down. Have you ever had clothes that literally grow on you? The length gets longer. Now, since there is a fixed amount of yarn in a swatch or sweater,

The potential growth of a swatch: gravity takes its toll

something's gotta give. If your piece is grow-
ing one way (lengthwise), it will compensate
by shrinking the other way (widthwise). (If
you are making an afghan or another project
that lies flat, this step is not necessary.)

Some fibers, including cotton, silk, and
rayon, are big culprits of this phenomenon.
What do they have in common? They are all
inelastic. The fibers have no memory, so
they will stretch out and not return to their
former shape.

Some other factors will also influence
growth. If you loosen up a gauge or use a hook
size much larger than called for, the struc-
tural integrity will be compromised and the
crocheted project will grow. Very heavy or
thick fabrics tend to do this as well. A garment
made with super-bulky yarn that weighs as
much as two or three pounds (0.9–1.4kg) can
be pulled down by its own weight.

This vertically grown gauge is known as a
hung gauge for obvious reasons. Let the
swatch hang for a day before measuring.
Take a "before" gauge with the swatch
lying flat to compare to the "after" gauges or
hung gauge, and note the difference. Your
work may come off the hook one size, but
after hanging it may become another. When
a pattern instructs you to "block pieces to
measurement," it means to let it grow to the

hung gauge. You can force this in the wet blocking process by wetting the fabric and pinning it to size but I prefer steam blocking (page 00). When directions state, "Work until piece measures 12 inches (30.5cm) from beginning," and you are working with a piece that showed a difference between the hung gauge and the flat gauge, don't work to that measurement. Instead, do the math and work to the hung row gauge. To do that, figure out how many rows will be worked in 12 inches (30.5cm), and count to that number of rows rather than relying on the measure-ment. Once you've factored in the growth and blocked it, the piece will be maxed out and should not grow any more.

● TIP HANGING IT UP

If the project I'm working on combines factors such as inelastic yarn or super-bulky yarn and a loosened gauge, I'll weigh down the swatch slightly with old-fashioned wooden clothespins or earrings or brooches to mimic the pull on a greater length of crocheted fabric. Let's say the garment is 24 inches (61cm) long in total. With a 6-inch (15cm) swatch, you will need the equivalent of three more swatches hanging from the bottom, for a total of four swatches, to represents the final length.

Weighing In

Now go weigh your swatch. I've been known
to go to the post office or the supermarket
where there are very accurate scales, but
you may have a food scale at home. Let's say
your 6-inch (15cm) swatch weighs ¼ ounce
(7g). Multiply three swatches by ¼ ounce (7g)
for a total weight of ¾ ounce (21g) pulling
down on your top swatch. Use the scale to
find out how many clothespins or earrings
or brooches make up ¾ ounce (21g). Hang
your swatch overnight with this amount of
weight evenly distributed across the bottom.
Take off the weights and let the swatch rest,
while still hanging, for a few hours. Now
take the swatch measurement.

6" x 6" swatch = 1/4 oz

1/4 oz
1/4 oz
1/4 oz

Weighing down
the swatch

The reason for hanging with stuff on, then
off, is to find the average. The second
swatch from the top only has two swatches,
or ½ ounce (14g) pulling it down. The second
from the bottom only has one swatch hanging from it, or ¼ ounce (7g). The very bottom
swatch has absolutely nothing hanging on
the bottom of it. Does it make sense to have
all and none for the average?

The real process, then, is to wash, block, and
hang. Again, I say wash, block, and hang. I
know this is not very spontaneous. I know all
too well how we all chomp at the bit to begin
a new project. However, there is a critical

line found on many directions, which usually appears under the gauge information: "To save time, take time to make the swatch." I'd amend it to say, "To save time, take time to make the swatch and to wash, block and hang it."

How Much Yarn Do You Need?

Sure you make a swatch to determine your tension or gauge, but the swatch can provide lots of other useful information, too. You know now that it will tell you about washability, wearability, and colorfastness of the yarn, and whether the knitted fabric will shrink or grow, but did you know it can also help you estimate your yarn needs?

Say you found a cute stitch in a stitch dictionary and want to create a simple piece without any shaping—a scarf or a stole or a blanket, for example—without using a pattern. How can you determine the amount of yarn you'll need? If you figure out about how big the finished piece will be, you can use the weight of your 6-inch (15cm) swatch to estimate the weight of the yarn you will need to complete the project. Start by folding a tablecloth, sheet, or piece of fabric to the width and length you want your scarf or shawl to be.

6" x 6" swatch
= 1/4 oz

Shawl

The number of swatches hanging in an imaginary garment

Scarf

Suppose you decide your scarf will be 12 inches (30.5cm) wide by 72 inches (183cm) long. How many 6-inch (15cm) square swatches will fit in your project? There will be an equivalent of two across by twelve down for a total of twenty-four swatches. If each swatch is $\frac{1}{4}$ ounce (7g), then twenty-four times $\frac{1}{4}$ ounce (7g) means 6 ounces (170g) of yarn is required for your scarf.

A shawl that is 18 inches (45.5cm) wide by 60 inches (152.5cm) long will require the equivalent of thirty swatches (three swatches across by ten down) at $\frac{1}{4}$ ounce (7g) per swatch, or 7 $\frac{1}{2}$ ounces (213g) of yarn. Can you figure out the yarn needed for an afghan measuring 48 inches (122cm) by 60 inches (152.5cm)? A food scale that can weigh the swatch in grams will give an even more accurate measurement of the weight. Swatching is now looking less like a tiresome chore, and more like a pretty useful exercise, isn't it?

YARN REQUIREMENTS FOR A SWEATER. When you're designing something more complex, like a sweater, take all the measurements you have in mind for the garment and apply the same principle. Let's say the sweater is 42 inches (106.5cm) wide overall—21 inches (53.5cm) each for the front and back—and 24 inches (61cm) long. The sleeves will be 18 inches (45.5cm) long, 9 inches (23cm) wide at the cuffs and 18 inches (45.5cm) wide at the top. Put all these measurements on a piece of square-grid graph paper (not knitting graph paper) where each box represents one inch (2.5 cm).

Now figure out how many 6-inch (15cm) square swatches fit into the sweater. Here's

Sweater
measurements
on graph paper

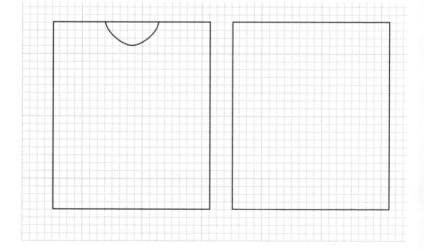

a quick way to do that, especially for the math-impaired. Just cut out several squares of the same graph paper that are six boxes by six boxes, lay them over the drawing of the sweater, and count! Keep careful track of how many boxes you use, and use the bits and pieces from the ones you cut to fit for the sleeves. This is a boon to the mathematically-impaired.

Here's the math. Seven swatches fit across both front and back pieces and four fit vertically for a total of twenty-eight 6-inch (15cm) swatches in the full body. For the sleeves, turn one sleeve upside down and place it next to the right-side-up sleeve to make a parallelogram. (A parallelogram

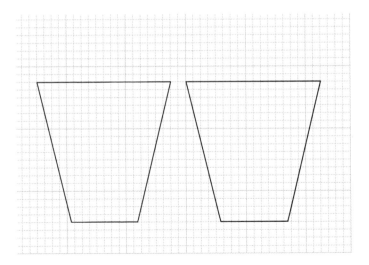

has the same formula for area as a rectangle, or height times width.)

This parallelogram is 27 inches (69cm) across (cuff plus top) or four-and-a-half swatches wide, and 18 inches (45.5cm) long, or three swatches vertically. So three times four-and-a-half equals thirteen-and-a-half swatches needed for both sleeves. Add this to the twenty-eight from the body and the entire sweater requires forty-one-and-a-half 6-inch (15cm) square swatches. Multiply this by the $1/4$ ounce (7g) per swatch and you get 10 $3/8$ ounces (294g) for the sweater.

You won't be crocheting a neck opening, so this formula will give you a little more yarn than you actually need, but that yarn may be used for the neckband. It's always good

Two sleeves: one turned upside down to create a parallelogram

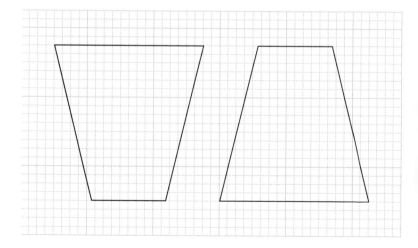

to have extra yarn just in case, so this estimate is pretty accurate.

Using Your Swatches

You can always find a use for the swatch.

- **Start a crocheting scrapbook.** Keep a record of the yarn and hook size, and if you are generous and give away a lot of pieces, take a picture of the finished item and keep it with the swatch.
- **When you crochet for others, give the swatch to recipients as a taste of things to come.** That baby blanket not finished? Well, give the swatch and promise that the blanket will be ready before the kid hits junior high school. Is your BFF's birthday sweater a bit late? Give her the swatch before she starts planning her next birthday party. If I can't get the gift out in a timely fashion, I'll give the swatch to show the recipient what's in store.
- **Use your swatches to make something new.** Collect your swatches and piece them together for a patchwork afghan or throw. Or fold the swatch in half, sew the sides together, and attach a small zipper to the top to make a coin purse.
- **Wash the swatch every time you launder the project** so you will always have matching yarn for mending the item later.

• **Do what most crocheters do with their swatches—rip out the yarn and use it in the project,** which is great especially if you run short. Most yarn can handle being gently ripped out and reused.

If you rip out your swatch to use the yarn again, you may need to straighten it out because the loops formed by crocheting have crimped the yarn. To remove these kinks, wind the yarn loosely in a hank (wrapping it around a stretched-out wire coat hanger works well), tie in several places (page 87), and then dunk the hank in water until it's thoroughly wet. Squeeze the water out and hang the hank until dry, then rewind. Do not weigh the yarn down to remove kinks; it can stretch out and result in yarn that won't have as much give as the rest of the balls of yarn, resulting in an uneven look after the next blocking.

Making a swatch helps you see how the yarn works up in a particular stitch and how much you enjoy crocheting with it. That stitch pattern may be very pretty to look at, but you may find that working it is a pain. Swatching allows you to sample the stitch pattern to see if you can live with it for the next several weeks. I call these the "trophy wife" stitches—pretty to look at but very high maintenance!

Adjusting Sweater Lengths

• •

The most flattering length of a sweater for
almost every body is one that hits at around
the hipbone. Often, the lengths given in a
pattern or set of instructions are not right
for us. For me, the right length is 20 inches
(51cm). To measure yourself, put a tape
measure at the highest point on the shoulder
(right next to the neck), and let it fall to the
hipbone—that's your preferred length.
An alternative is to take any garment whose
length you like and measure that.

Now you can make the adjustments to the
pattern according to your length. Almost
all patterns today come with an illustrated
set of measurements called a schematic.
Choose the size you want to make and
draw those measurements on graph paper,
with each box equal to one inch (2.5cm).
Do this in pencil so that you can erase any
errors later.

All adjustments to length—one of the
easiest changes to make to a pattern—
should occur below the armholes. That way,
the armholes stay the same and the sleeve
will still fit into them. Make the changes to
the schematic for your length so you now
know how long to make the body before you
have to begin the armhole shaping.

A pattern's schematics drawn on graph paper

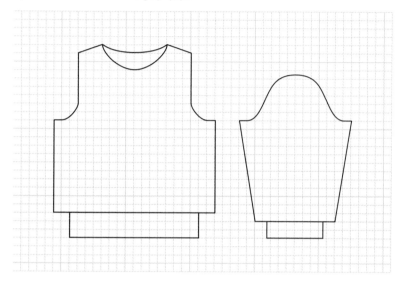

A pattern's schematics adjusted for length

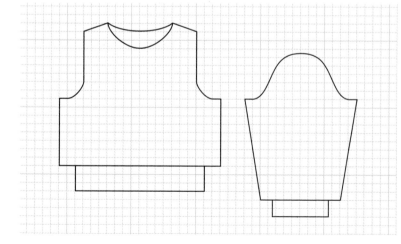

But wait, there's more. Most patterns call for a standard three inches (7.5cm) of ribbing on the body and two inches (5cm) of ribbing for the sleeves. Does this have to be the case? Of course not. You can make changes to the ribbing too. Experiment with proportions that please your eye. Go for a modern high-waisted ribbing to create the Empire line or go for minimal ribs for a more funky look. The proportions are up to you. Just keep in mind that the ribbing also works to keep the edges from curling and there may be a minimum needed to keep the edges from flipping up. You can crochet a swatch with ribbing to see how it works. Remember

Standard ribbing

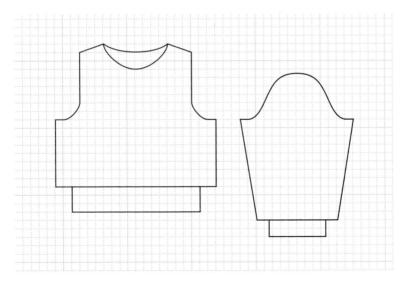

Changes to ribbing proportions

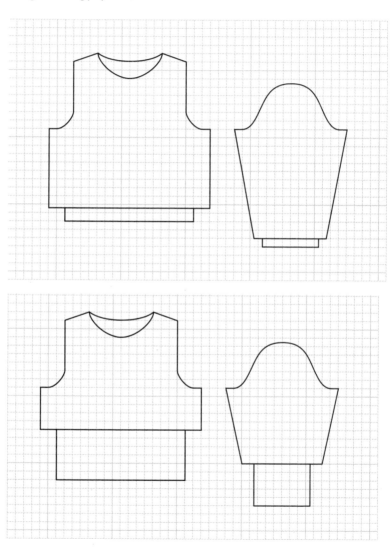

that adjustments to sleeve length mean refiguring how often to increase (for example, every fourth row so many times, then every sixth row so many times, and so on).

● **TIP** FINDING THE #%^!$#@%~ CENTER OF A BALL OF YARN

We all prefer to have what is known as a center-pull skein so that the ball of yarn does not roll around as we work. Unfortunately, the center strand is not always evident and we have to fish inside the skein for it, usually ending up pulling out a huge wad of yarn that's almost half the skein.

To find the center more easily, go in from either end of the ball. Insert your fingers into the top and bottom of the skein, almost like Chinese handcuffs. When your fingers meet, you know you're in the center. Now twirl a finger around and feel for the inner spiral, grab the yarn closest to the inside, and pull it out. You should be able to pull out just a pinch of yarn.

Using your fingers to find the center of a ball of yarn

Working with Coned Yarns

Coned yarns are a lot more economical to use than skeins. I love the fact that with a cone you don't need to join separate skeins, and as a result end up with fewer ends to weave in. Since coned yarns are most often used for machine knitting the yarns are sometimes treated with wax to smooth stray fibers and flatten the plies to facilitate movement through the machine. The yarn is under tension as it is wound onto a cone, so by the time it gets to the crocheter, it's is often flattened and stretched out.

If you crochet with coned yarns as is, you will see a remarkable transformation when you wash your swatch (and you do swatch, don't you?). The wax washes away, the yarn springs back, and the swatch fluffs up to fill empty spaces. Some yarns that appear very limp and lifeless are transformed into something wonderfully soft and springy.

To wash or not to wash. If you wash the yarn before you crochet with it, you will have the softer and springier yarn to work with rather than the stringier and less-than-satisfying off-the-cone feeling. To do this, wind the yarn into hanks around the back of a chair and tie it in at least four evenly

A yarn hank tied in
several places

spaced places with smooth, contrasting
cotton. Now wash the yarn as you would the
finished product and let it dry flat and
unstretched. Rewind the yarn into a ball
either by hand or by using a yarn winder.
I know, you're saying that there are too
many extra steps and you want to begin the
project already. Did I tell you how awfully
soft prewashed cashmere can be compared
to the limp and unwashed version?

● **TIP** SETTING UP CONED YARN
If you are going to use coned yarn straight
from the cone, which works well with
cotton, reeling the yarn off the cone is often
problematic, since pulling on it sideways
usually results in the cone toppling over.
You can use a floor lamp and have the yarn
feed upward first, then horizontally over

the lamp. Or try a small lazy Susan so that the yarn feeds off horizontally when the lazy Susan spins around.

GOING CONELESS. I often push the cardboard cone out to make the yarn almost like a large center-pull ball. To do this, I sit in a chair and place the upside-down cone on the floor between my feet. I push downward with my feet as I pull the cardboard cone up and out of the yarn. If it doesn't come out easily, sometimes I try to pull the cone out with pliers or I may hammer down on the cone from the top. If all else fails, I just use the floor lamp setup.

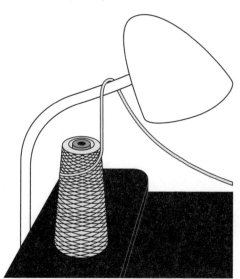

Coned yarn coming up over a lamp for better feeding

A Better Beginning Foundation Chain

• •

Inevitably, almost every crocheter finds that the beginning foundation chains are way too tight. This is because splitting the chain open in order to go through the top two strands pulls up on the length of the chain. If you go through the top strand only, it pulls up less but you're left with a stitch that has a weak hold to the chain. Such is the bane and scourge of the chain.

The easiest way to avoid the too-tight chain is to use a hook one or two sizes larger than the one you'll use for the rest of the crocheting. Just don't forget to change back to the smaller hook after finishing the chain. (Guess how I know?)

If you're working a looser gauge than normal, that is, you're using a larger hook relative to the yarn thickness, the use of an even larger hook for the foundation chain can prove problematic. The chain either becomes so loose that it's hard to find the place to insert the hook or it winds up being way too flimsy. Try using two strands of yarn held together for the chain. If this is too thick (I know, the Goldilocks syndrome), split the plies of the yarn and use one-and-a-half strands for the chain.

If the piece you are crocheting will eventually be seamed, you may want to reel off some seaming yarn before forming the slip knot of the chain.

Going Through the Back Bump

My favorite way of going into the foundation chain is not to go under the usual top two strands of the chain. Instead, rotate the chain until you see the back bump of the chain (it looks like a purl stitch in knitting) and insert the hook into the bump.

By working into this back bump, the full chain remains in view at the bottom of the work, and will match the top edge of any crochet stitch. This is important in an item like a scarf where both ends are in view, and you want the top and bottom to match.

This technique is also helpful when you want to go into the underside of the chain later to put on a trim or to lengthen a piece that's too short. Furthermore, it forms the smoothest bottom and who wouldn't like a smoother bottom?

Going through the back bump of a chain

● **TIP** CHAINING ONTO A KNITTING NEEDLE

The one drawback to working into the back bump is that fishing for that pesky bump can be difficult. Not only is it be hard to find, it can also be too tight to work into. My solution is to use a knitting needle about the same size as the hook (page 16).

Start with the slip knot on the hook. With the hook in the right hand and a knitting needle in the left, bring the yarn behind the needle from below and to front from above the needle. Catch the yarn with the hook and pull it through to form a chain. Repeat this yarn-around-needle before every chain until you will have as many loops on the needle as you have chains. This places the back bump of the chain on the knitting needle, and there's no need to hunt for it.

After chaining the required number, make a turning chain (page 48): chain one for single crochet or two for half double crochet or three for double crochet without

Working a chain over a knitting needle

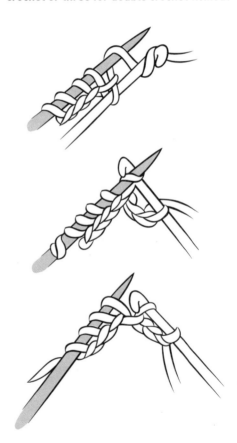

wrapping the yarn around needle, then
work into the back bumps by inserting the
hook into a loop on the needle and taking
it off at the same time. This method of
chaining is great for textured or dark yarns.

Counting the Chains

The problem with having to complete the
foundation chain before you start the rows of
stitches is that you often don't quite have the
correct number. You thought you counted
correctly, but it turns out you're off. Having
too many is much better than having too few
because you can always snip away the
excess later and weave in the ends. To help
in counting, I put markers every twenty chains
or so. I use plastic mini–diaper pins, coilless
safety pins, split-ring markers, and even
bobby pins or bits of scrap yarn as markers.

● **TIP** GAINING EXTRA STITCHES

If your project requires a humongous
number of chains, say 250, and you run out
of chains, don't rip out and start again.
I have a solution. If you need more chains,
you can add more. Make a slip knot with a
separate strand of the same yarn. Insert the
crochet hook into the chain next to the beginning slip knot of the original chain, place
the newly formed slip knot onto the hook

from front to back, and pull the slip knot through to the front. Now continue to make more chains, as many as needed, with this new strand of yarn, then cut it and end off the new strand. This is not a perfect solution. The new chain runs the opposite direction from the original, and you have two extra ends to weave in later. However, it's much better than ripping out and having to start over.

Adding stitches
to a chain

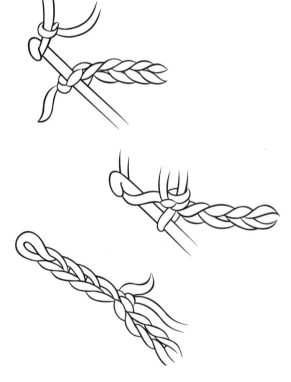

Working the Stitch and Chain Simultaneously

Often called the foundationless chain or chainless stitch, this method of creating the chain at the same time you work the stitch was popularized by Mary Rhodes of California. I've been told that this technique appeared in crochet pamphlets from Coats and Clark in the 1950s, but Mary is the one who turned me on to it. This method creates a solid row of stitches, and is not usually meant for lace. See http://www.baycrochet.com/foundatn.htm for more on this technique.

Chainless Single Crochet

Begin with the slip knot, then chain 2. Insert the hook under two strands of the second chain from hook and pick up a loop. There are now two loops on the hook. Yarn over and draw through the two loops. One single crochet has been made.

Chainless
single crochet

Insert the hook under the front two strands of the stitch you just made and pick up a loop. There are now two loops on the hook. Yarn around the hook and pull the yarn through only one loop on the hook. This forms the "chain" part of the next stitch. Place your thumb on this so-called chain as it will be where you'll insert the hook later. There are still two loops on the hook. Yarn around the hook and pull through both remaining loops on the hook to complete the single crochet itself. The second single crochet has been made.

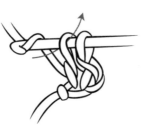
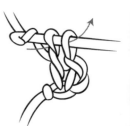

*See where your thumb is? You will now go under two strands of this so-called chain and pick up a loop—there are now two loops on the hook. Yarn around the hook and pull the yarn through only one loop on the hook. This forms the "chain" part of the stitch. Place your thumb on this so-called chain as it will be where you'll insert the hook later. There are still two loops on the hook. Yarn around the hook and pull through both remaining loops on the hook to complete the next single crochet *. Repeat between the *s until the piece is the desired length.

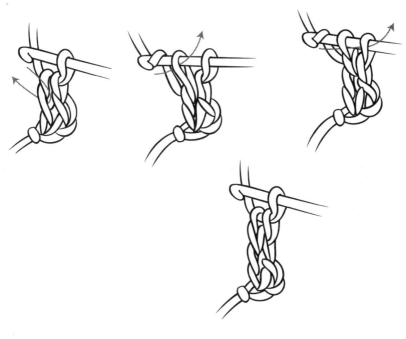

Chainless Half Double Crochet

Working a chainless half double crochet is very much like a chainless single crochet but with an extra loop. Again, begin with the slip knot, then chain 3. Yarn around the hook first, then insert the hook under two strands of the third chain from the hook and pick up a loop—there are now three loops on the hook. This looks like the start of a half double crochet. Now yarn around the hook as though to complete the half double crochet, but pull the yarn through only one loop on the hook. This forms the "chain" part of the stitch. Place your thumb on this so-called chain; it will be where you'll insert the hook later. Notice how there are still three loops on the hook. Now yarn around the hook and pull through all three loops on the hook to complete the half double crochet itself.

See where your thumb is? * Yarn around the hook and go under two strands of this so-called chain and pick up a loop— there are now three loops on the hook. Now yarn around the hook as you would to complete the half double crochet but pull the yarn through only one loop on the hook. This forms the "chain" part of the stitch. Place your thumb on this so-called chain. There are three loops left on the hook. Yarn around the hook and pull through all three loops on the hook to complete the half double crochet itself *. Repeat between the *s until the piece is the desired length.

Chainless Double Crochet

By now, I think you can figure out how to work a chainless double crochet, but I'll walk you through it anyway. It starts much like a chainless half double crochet. Again, begin with the slip knot, then chain 4. Yarn around the hook first, then insert the hook under two strands of the fourth chain from the hook and pick up a loop—there are now three loops on the hook. This looks like the start of a double crochet. Now yarn around the hook as if you're ready to complete the double crochet, but pull the yarn through only one loop on the hook. This forms the "chain" part of the stitch. Place your thumb on this so-called chain; it will be where you'll insert the hook later. There are still three loops on the hook. Now [yarn around the hook and pull through two loops on the hook] twice to complete the double crochet itself. See where your thumb is? * Yarn around the hook and go under two strands of this so-called chain and pick up a loop—there are now three loops on the hook. Yarn around the hook as if you're ready to complete the double crochet but pull the yarn through only one loop on the hook. This forms the "chain" part of the stitch. Place your thumb on this so-called chain. There are still three loops on the hook. Now [yarn around the hook and pull through two loops on the hook] twice to complete the double crochet itself *. Repeat between the *s until the piece is the desired length.

Chainless Treble Crochet

The chainless treble crochet follows the same pattern. Once more, begin with the slip knot, then chain 5. Yarn around the hook first, then insert the hook under two strands of the fifth chain from the hook and pick up a loop—there are now four loops on the hook. This looks like the start of a treble crochet. Now yarn around the hook as though to complete the treble crochet but pull the yarn through only one loop on the hook. This forms the "chain" part of the stitch. Place your thumb on this so-called chain; it will be where you'll insert the hook later. There are four loops left on the hook. Now [yarn around the hook and pull through two loops on the hook] three times to complete the treble crochet itself. See where your thumb is? * Yarn around the hook and go under two strands of this so-called chain and pick up a loop—there are now three loops on the hook. Yarn around the hook as if you're ready to complete the treble crochet but pull the yarn through only one loop on the hook. This forms the "chain" part of the stitch. Place your thumb on this so-called chain. There are four loops left on the hook. Now [yarn around the hook and pull through two loops on the hook] three times to complete the treble crochet itself *. Repeat between the *s until the piece is the desired length.

Chainless crochet creates a looser and more flexible foundation chain. Using it, you never run out of chains or have any leftover chains at the end. This method is great when you want to add several stitches at the end of a row. Since the yarn is at the beginning of a row, you can chain at the beginning to add several stitches.

Skipping Over Chains to Create Filet Mesh

In many stitch patterns—especially lace—skipping over and not working into a certain number of chains is part of the design. The most common and easiest form of lace is called filet mesh. In the basic filet mesh pattern, you * work a double crochet in the next chain, chain 2, skip two chains, and then repeat from the *. This forms an open grid.

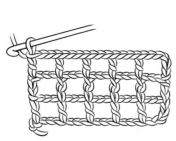

Filet mesh

If you accidentally skip only one chain or skip over three chains instead of two, you'll end up with either too many or too few chains at the end, and the result will be a wonky, lopsided mesh. The chain can also twist around and be uneven at the bottom edge. So I suggest not crocheting into a foundation chain at all.

How is this possible? In knitting, there is a technique called a temporary or provisional cast-on, in which a length of waste yarn is used to establish the stitches and then is torn out later. And I thought why can't crocheters do the same thing?

USING A PROVISIONAL CHAIN. Inspired by the knitted cast-on, I worked out a provisional chain. To do this, use a smooth cotton yarn about the same weight as the working yarn.

I like cotton because it seldom frays. This yarn will be the provisional or temporary chain—you work over the cotton as if it were the foundation chain. Use a length of cotton a bit longer than the project's width. If you're making a 16-inch (40.5cm) wide shawl, reel off about 20 inches (51cm) of waste yarn. Tie huge knots on either end of the waste cotton by making knots over knots, and put it aside.

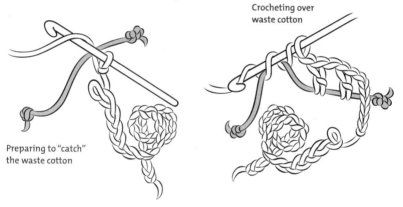

Crocheting over waste cotton

Preparing to "catch" the waste cotton

Now working with the real yarn, make a chain as long as called for in the instructions, plus several extra inches. Wad up this chain into a ball, being careful not to lose the last chain. Make a slip knot after the last chain and place it on the hook. Place the piece of waste-cotton over the working yarn and chain 5 (this counts as a double crochet and a chain-2).

As you work the first chain, the working yarn will catch the waste yarn. Now *work a double crochet around the waste yarn as if it were a chain, chain 2, repeat from the * several times. End with a double crochet around the waste yarn. Now continue working on the filet mesh. For practice, work a row or two of filet mesh by working a double crochet in each double crochet and chain-2 over each chain-2 space. Fasten and end off. The large knots at each end of the waste yarn will prevent the stitches from falling off. Turn the work upside down and insert the hook into the underside of the first chain.

Beginning the underside of the first chain

Place the yarn from the wadded-up chain over the hook and draw a loop through. This creates the chain that the first double crochet would have gone into. Chain 2 to create the first skipped-over chain of the

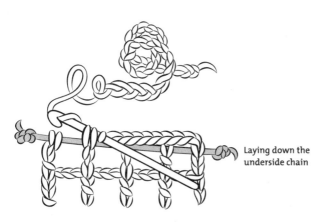

Laying down the underside chain

foundation. * Insert the hook into both loops of the underside of the next double crochet, yarn around the hook, and make a slip stitch: This creates the chain that this double crochet would have gone into. Chain 2 to create the next skipped-over chain of the foundation. Repeat from the * across, undoing the original chain to provide working yarn as needed. Work a slip stitch into the underside of the last double crochet, fasten and end off.

The bottom of each double crochet is made up of two loops. By laying in the foundation chain afterwards in this manner, it will not be too tight. The bottom of the piece matches the top edge, and the foundation chain is never twisted. There will always be the correct number of chains at the start, and you will never skip over too many or too few chains. To finish, snip off one knot of the waste-cotton and pull it out. You now also know why you started with the chain wadded up into a ball—to know the exact amount of yarn required for the foundation chain.

● **TIP** CROCHETING AROUND A KNITTING NEEDLE

Although waste-cotton is readily available, it tends to flop around as you work over it. For more stability, try crocheting over the thin nylon cable of a circular knitting needle. Crochet around the thin, nylon cable in the middle. The needle ends act as the knot or stopper, and still allows the stitches to slide off when necessary.

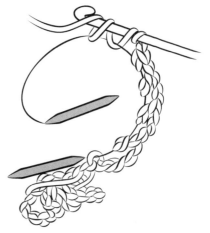

Crocheting
over a circular
knitting needle

Lace Patterns in Symbols

The Japanese are pioneers of the international system of charting patterns. They found that using symbols for stitches rather than writing out the instructions saves both space and repetition. Symbols also transcend the language barrier so anyone can understand the patterns, and they are also a great visualizing tool. You can see what has to be done, where the piece is going, and where it has been, because you have a picture of the stitches to be worked.

Stitch Key

Term	Symbol
chain (ch) =	⬭
slip stitch (sl st) =	•
single crochet (sc) =	+
double crochet (dc) =	⊤

V-STITCH LACE PATTERN. In a V-stitch lace, you work two double crochet stitches into the same chain. The chart of this pattern shows a beginning chain of thirty-four. Row 1 reads as (double crochet, chain 1, double crochet) all in the seventh chain from the hook, * skip three chains, (double crochet, chain 1, double crochet) all in the next chain; repeat from the * across, end by skipping two chains and making a double crochet in the last chain. On subsequent rows, you work a V-stitch (double crochet, chain 1, double crochet) in the same chain-1 space of the previous V-stitch.

Notice how the stitches do not form V's at first when worked over either waste yarn or a circular knitting needle. Instead, they read straight up and down as (double crochet, chain 1, double crochet) across. When laying down the chain later, the hook goes into the underside of two double crochet (four loops total) in the slip stitch that links them to-

(top)
V-stitch chart

(bottom)
Double crochet stitches; not yet V-stitches, when worked over waste-cotton or circular knitting needle

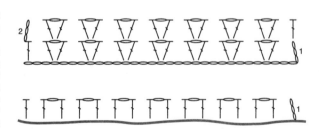

gether. So after joining the yarn to the underside of the first chain, chain 2, * slip stitch into the underside of the next two double crochet together, chain 3; then repeat from the * across, ending with chain 2, slip stitch in the underside of the last double crochet.

SHELL STITCH LACE PATTERN. In this lace pattern, you work four double crochet into the same chain. The chart begins with chain 47. On row 1, work (2 double crochet, chain 1, 2 double crochet) in the eighth chain from the hook, * skip four chains, work (2 double crochet, chain 1, 2 double crochet) in the next chain; repeat from the * across, and end by skipping three chains and making a double crochet in the last chain. On subsequent rows, you work a shell stitch (2 double crochet, chain 1, 2 double crochet) in the same chain-1 space of the previous shell stitch.

Notice how the stitches do not form shells at first when worked over either waste yarn

(top)
Shell stitch chart

(bottom)
Double crochet stitches; not yet Shell stitches, when worked over waste cotton or circular knitting needle

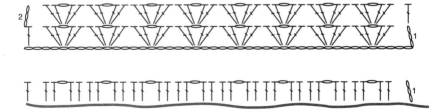

or a circular knitting needle. Instead, they read straight up and down as (2 double crochet, chain 1, 2 double crochet) across. When laying down the chain later, the hook goes into the underside of four double crochet (eight loops total) in the slip stitch that links them together. So after joining the yarn to the underside of the first chain, chain 3, * slip stitch into the underside of the next four double crochet stitches together, chain 4; then repeat from the * across, ending with chain 3, slip stitch into the underside of the last double crochet.

SCALLOP STITCH PATTERN. In this pattern, five double crochet are worked into the same chain. The chart begins with chain 32. On row 1, single crochet in the second chain from the hook, * skip two chains, 5 double crochet in the next chain, skip two chains, single crochet in the next chain; repeat from the * across.

The stitches will not form shells when worked over either waste yarn or a circular knitting needle. Instead, they read straight up and down as (single crochet, 5 double crochet) across. When laying down the chain later, the hook goes into the underside of five double crochet (ten loops total) in the slip stitch that links them together. So after joining the yarn to the underside of the first chain, slip stitch into the underside of the first single crochet, * chain 2, slip stitch into the underside of the next 5 double crochet together, chain 2, slip stitch into the underside of the next single crochet; repeat from the * across.

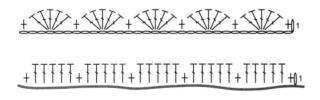

(top)
Scallop stitch chart

(bottom)
Double crochet stitches; not yet Scallop stitches, when worked over waste cotton or circular knitting needle

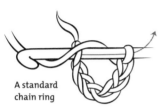

A standard
chain ring

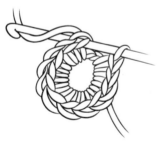

Working in a Circle

When working in a circle, the standard way
to begin is to chain three, four, five, or six,
then join to the first chain (by the slip knot)
with a slip stitch. For the next row, you chain
according to the stitch height and work
several stitches into this newly formed ring.

Another method is to chain equal to the
stitch height plus one extra, and then work
all the stitches into the last chain (by the slip
knot) or the very first chain worked.

● **TIP** WORKING INTO A SLIP KNOT

**In the standard methods of working into a
chain loop or into one chain stitch, the ring
is either so large, it leaves an ungainly gap
in the fabric or so tight that it is difficult to
squeeze in the required number of stitches.
My solution is rather simple. Begin by
making a slip knot (page 44), leaving a 6-inch
(15cm) tail, where the slip knot end opens
and closes. If you pull on the tail, the loop
should get smaller, and if you open up the
loop, the tail gets shorter.**

Open up the slip knot a bit. This loop of the slip knot is now your ring, and is used instead of a series of chains joined by a slip stitch. Begin working into the loop by inserting the hook through the center, grabbing the yarn, and bringing a new loop forward.

Chain according to the stitch height and work several stitches into this newly formed ring. The beauty of this slip knot as ring is that you can open it up to accommodate a large number of stitches, and can still pull it closed so you aren't left with a gaping hole. (In fact, it closes to almost a pinhole.) To finish, thread the tail onto a darning or tapestry needle, make a French knot on the back of the work to prevent the hole from opening up again, and weave in the tail.

Working into a slip knot

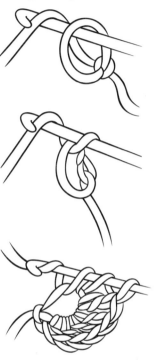

A tightly
closed circle

● **TIP** A MAGIC RING

A magic ring uses an untightened knot of
sorts. Begin with a loop, insert the hook into
this loop from front to back, grab the yarn,
and bring a new loop forward.

Chain according to the stitch height and
work several stitches into this newly
formed ring, working over the tail as well.
This ring, which has become popular as of
late, is adjustable in size. I have found that it
does not open back up very smoothly. Try
the magic ring and working into a slip knot
and decide which method works for you.

Working into a
loose knot

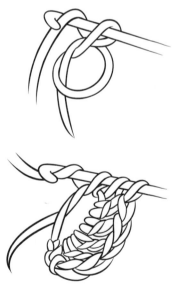

● **TIP** WORKING WITH BIGGER CIRCLES

When working on a large project in the round, such as a poncho or a seamless garment body, you will make a long chain. The directions will tell you to join the chain on the hook to the last chain next to the slip knot with a slip stitch, being careful not to twist the chain around. Easier said than done. With a long chain, how do you prevent the twist? I use wooden clothespins and work on a large pillow on my lap.

Every so many chains, let's say twenty or twenty-five, place a clothespin on the chain with the front side facing up. Arrange the chain in hairpin turns to take up less space. At the end, work toward the beginning, check that all clothespins have the front of the chain facing up, and then join with a slip stitch.

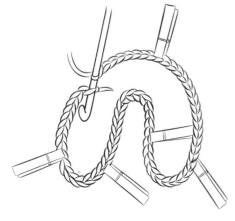

Joining a large
circle without
twisting the chain

In This Chapter

As You Work

As you crochet, there will inevitably be some bumps along the way. Perhaps you've just run out of yarn, maybe the instructions aren't totally clear. The **hints and tips** in this chapter will provide the tools for you to **smooth over** some of those bumps so you can sit back and **enjoy** your crocheting!

Joining New Yarn

At some point, you will have to introduce a new ball or skein. You may run out of yarn and or need to introduce a new color when working stripes. In either case, try to make this change at the edges of the piece or the beginning or end of a row.

Joining the
new yarn the
traditional way

Most of us were taught to add in the new yarn (either a new color or more of the same yarn) by starting right in with the new stuff, leaving ample tail to weave in later. I don't know about you, but I always get rather nervous about this. I have visions of the whole thing unraveling and it seems to me that the last stitch of the old ball and the first stitch of the new one are always loose, sloppy, and ungainly. And how annoying is it to accidentally start to work with the long end rather than with they yarn from the ball?

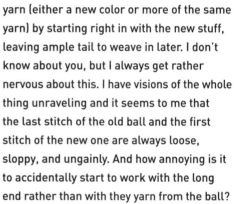

Joining the new
yarn in the last step
of the stitch

A BETTER WAY. There is a better way to do this. For starters, don't switch yarns at the turning chains. Instead, as with colorwork, work off the last two loops of the stitch you are working on (the last three loops of half double crochet) with the new yarn. This will bury the new yarn under these last two (or three) loops.

Second, don't just let those ends dangle—tie one on. No, vodka is not involved. Just wrap the new yarn around the old one and tie a simple knot. The knot of new yarn should slide up and down the old yarn. Snuggle the yarn up close to the stitch, work off the last two loops with the new yarn, and then continue working with the new yarn.

Tying the new yarn around the old one

"Knot" only will this prevent raveling while you work, but the stitches will be set in there nicely and firmly. If the thought of any knots at all bothers you, not to worry. This knot is the simplest you can make and, after completing the project, you can easily take it out and weave in the end. If you prefer to leave it, that's not a problem either. The knot isn't bulky and since it's at the edge, hide it in the trim or in a seam. Another advantage to knotting the yarn is that the tail does not need to be excessively long—you'll never mistake the tail for the working end.

● **TIP** MEASURING YARN FOR ONE ROW

How do you know if you have enough yarn to make it to the end of the row? As you approach the end of the yarn ball, start keeping track of exactly how many yards you need to make one row. Reel off five to ten yards (4.5m to 9m) at a time and place a slip

knot on the yarn to mark the reeled-off yardage. On a piece of paper, use old-fashioned ticks or hash marks to keep track of how many yards have been reeled off.

This tip will also help you out toward the end of your project. If you're running out of yarn, you can now project how many more rows are necessary before you complete the project and how much yarn that entails. If you see that there is not enough yarn left, either go to the store immediately to buy more or find some other solution, such as trimming in another color or another yarn.

● **TIP** SPIT SPLICING

If you are using a yarn that can be felted (pure wool, for example), you can use a technique known as the spit splice. As the name implies, you felt the two ends of yarn together, by spitting on them and rapidly rolling them together between the palms of your hands. If this does not sound palatable, use warm water—adding a little soap is even better. I like to fray the ends for two to three inches (5cm to 7.5cm) first to ensure good contact. I then remove about half the amount of fiber from each frayed end so that when they're combined, the two ends are the same thickness as one strand of yarn. I then try to intertwine the remaining ends,

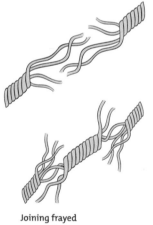

Joining frayed
yarn ends

wet them, and then roll them. This technique is best used for same-colored yarns because finding the exact point where one should change colors is too tricky. Make the splice several yards before you need it to allow the ends to dry. Never spit splice after drinking coffee or red wine, for obvious reasons.

● **TIP** NEEDLE FELTING

If you are using yarn that can't be felted (a synthetic or superwash wool, for example), you can use needle felting to create a join similar to spit splicing. I've used this method with great success on manmade fibers and cotton; I've yet to try it on rayon and silk. To do this, you will need a felting needle—a long, very sharp needle with barbs at one end—and something protective like a thick piece of foam to place under the work so that you don't jab into the table or your thigh! Fray, halve, and intertwine the yarn ends as you did for spit splicing, then punch the needle up and down through the yarn repeatedly, which drives the fibers through each other, causing them to adhere together. The results are a bit fuzzy, but I cut off the fuzzy bits. This makes a surprisingly strong hold that works best on yarn of the same color.

The Russian join

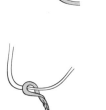

● **TIP** THE RUSSIAN JOIN

Another alternative for joining yarns is the Russian join. Here the two yarn ends loop around each other, then each takes a U-turn and is woven into itself with a tapestry or darning needle. Halve or thin out both ends, as described in spit splicing, for about four inches (10cm).

Begin with one yarn, threading the halved end onto a darning needle and weaving it onto the yarn itself, forming a small loop. Leave a little bit of the halved end accessible. Thread the other yarn end through the loop of the first yarn and use the needle to weave this yarn into itself, leaving a small loop. Now pull on the halved tail ends of each yarn to close up both loops. Trim off the remaining halved tail ends.

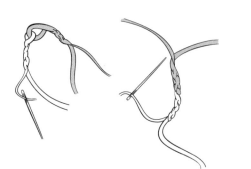

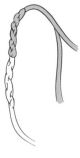

● **TIP** WORKING WITH RIBBON YARN

Ribbon yarns are so pretty in the skein, but seem to totally lose their flat, smooth texture when they are crocheted. This is partially due to the twisting of the ribbon as it comes off the ball. It's irritating, but easily fixed. Does toilet paper ever twist? No. Apply the same principle to dispenser ribbon yarn and you'll alleviate some of this twisting. To make a ribbon dispenser, take an old shoebox and a straight knitting needle of any size. Pierce the outside of the shoebox with the needle, place the ball of ribbon onto the needle, then pierce the other side of the shoebox so that the ribbon hangs inside the shoebox.

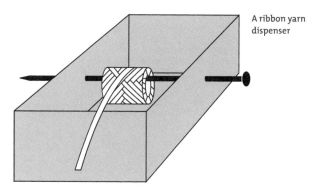

A ribbon yarn dispenser

● **TIP** JOINING RIBBON YARNS

When joining the ends of ribbon yarn, even the smallest knots will be too bulky. I overlap the ends of ribbon together by about ⅛ inch (3mm) and sew them together with matching sewing thread and needle for an imperceptible, bulk-free joining. With this method there are no ends to weave in (important since ribbons tend to be slippery), no waste (great since ribbon tends to be pricey), and the sewing stitches will help prevent fraying at the ribbon ends.

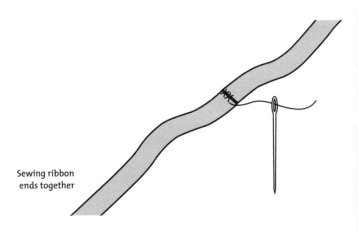

Sewing ribbon
ends together

Making Stripes

One of the easiest ways to dress up a project is to change colors every few rows to create horizontal stripes. (To add a new color yarn, see page 118.) When changing colors at any time, always work off the last two loops of any stitch (the last three loops of half double crochet) with the next color. If the stripes are narrow—that is, if you change colors every two or four rows—don't cut the color not being used, simply carry it up along the side edge. This forms a short float of the nonworking yarn. Do not pull these floats up too tightly or the edge will bunch up and become distorted. Conversely, don't leave them too loose or the edge will be sloppy.

Stripes are usually worked in even-num-bered row combinations. That's because you must get back to the same edge where the other yarn is waiting to be used next. If you are working circularly, however, the stripes can occur in odd-numbered increments.

Floats along the side of a striped piece

● **TIP** HIDING LONG FLOATS

On taller stitches, such as double crochet, the floats will be longer. Longer stripes of six or eight rows or more create floats that are too long and will catch and snag. But ending off the yarn and rejoining means

Hiding floats along
the side edge

more ends to weave in and no one wants
that. The solution is to catch the yarn not
being used at that edge of the work.

To do that, just lay the nonworking yarn
over the working yarn before beginning the
new row. When you chain for the following
row, this catches the float in the side edge.
You can lay the nonworking yarn from front
to back or from back to front, just keep it
consistent. Now you can work stripes of six
or eight rows—even twelve or twenty-four
rows—without ever having to end off and
reattach yarns. You'll also be left with very
few ends to weave in. Check the tension
of the floats as you work so the edge does
not become distorted.

Changing Colors Mid-row

Intarsia (also known as picture crochet) and color blocks both require changing colors in the middle of a row. Leaving a knot in the middle of your work is never a good idea, but go ahead and tie on the new yarn color (page 119). You can untie the knot later and weave in the ends. As with stripes, always work off the last two loops of the old color with the new color.

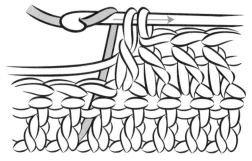

Changing colors
mid-row

Chaining at the Beginning of a Row

Even if you're an advanced beginner, turning chains while working back and forth in rows can be confusing. While a chain-2 replaces the first stitch in half double crochet, a chain-3 replaces the first stitch in double crochet, and a chain-4 replaces the first stitch in treble crochet, the chain-1 at the beginning of the row in single crochet does not substitute for the first stitch. That is, after chaining one stitch, you still work a single crochet into the first stitch at the beginning of the row.

I truly despise that extra space this creates at the beginning of half double crochet and double crochet rows. The gap becomes even more evident after seaming or adding trim. That chain-2 or chain-3 isn't fooling anyone. The chains are much more flimsy than a regular half double or double crochet stitch and who enjoys working into the top chain at the end of the rows? Not me.

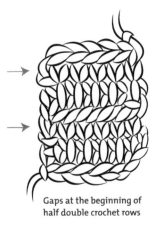

Gaps at the beginning of
half double crochet rows

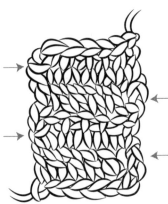

Gaps at the beginning of
double crochet rows

● TIP AVOIDING SPACE AT THE
BEGINNING OF A ROW

To avoid this space at the beginning of
half double and double crochet rows, I use a
loosened, elongated chain that does not
count as a stitch, just as in single crochet. To
work this, loosen the loop that's on the hook
slightly, work a loose chain, and then loosen
the loop that's on the hook slightly.

This method gets the work to the proper
height of the stitch(es) to be worked on that
row. Because it does not take the place of
the first stitch and the first stitch is worked
into the first stitch of the previous row, there
is no space.

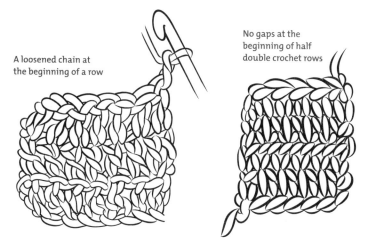

A loosened chain at
the beginning of a row

No gaps at the
beginning of half
double crochet rows

No gaps at the
beginning of
double crochet
rows

While there is a bit more "stuff" at the side edges every other row, it is minimal since it is a single, loosened chain. And when seaming or applying trim, it is a big plus not to have the gaping spaces. The best part is that you do not have to work into the top of a chain-3 (or chain-2 of half double crochet) at the end of the rows; just leave the loosened chain-1 alone.

Some crocheters work a single crochet-chain-2 into the first stitch in double crochet rows. This does close up the gap somewhat, but the chain at the top is still flimsy and you still have to work into the top of this chain on subsequent later rows.

Joining Rounds

When working circularly, another kind of gap develops. At the end of each round, most crocheters use a slip stitch to join the last stitch of the first round to the first stitch of the next round. This stitch, small as it is, leaves a little space (seen here in single crochet, half double crochet, and double crochet) and it bothers me.

If you turn the work after joining to work the next row, you skip over the slip stitch, leaving yet another gap. This is most evident in taller stitches, such as double crochet, but even joins in single crochet have an odd, irregular blip called a jog.

Gaps in rounds of double crochet

Gaps in rounds of single crochet

Gaps in rounds of half double crochet

● **TIP** AVOIDING THE SLIP STITCH JOG

Here are two ways to avoid that slip stitch jog. First, instead of joining with a slip stitch, try joining the last stitch to the top of the first stitch. To do that, work to within the last two loops as you would do a color change (the last three loops of half double crochet), insert the hook into the top of the first stitch, then yarn around the hook and go through all the loops—the top of the first stitch as well as the remaining two or three loops on the hook. When worked with a loosened chain on double crochet and half double crochet, this creates an almost gap-free join. The blips are less noticeable as well. Another way to avoid the slip stitch jog

A smooth join in rows of single crochet

A smooth join in rows of half double crochet

A smooth join in rows of double crochet

involves dropping the loop from the hook.
Complete the last stitch, and then drop
the loop from the hook. Insert the hook into
the first stitch from the wrong side to the
right side, place the loop back onto
the hook, and draw this loop through the
first stitch. When you are working a right-
side row, the hook goes from back to front.
When you are working a wrong-side row,
the hook goes from the front to the back.
There is even less of a gap to this method,
but there will be a slight seam on the back
of the work. Also, dropping the loop from
the hook and picking it up again does
interrupt the flow of the crocheting. Since
the first method is a little faster, doesn't

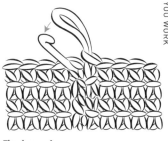

The dropped-
loop join

A dropped-loop join
in double crochet

A dropped-loop join
in single crochet

A dropped-loop
join in half double
crochet

Traditional single crochet decrease

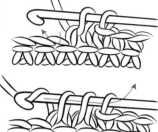

Traditional half double crochet decrease

interfere with the rhythm of the work, and leaves no seam along the back, it's preferred when making a reversible piece. There is also slightly less bulk. Try both methods to see which you like better.

A Better Decrease for Single Crochet and Half Double Crochet

One quick and easy way to decrease a stitch is to just skip over it and not work it. However, this creates a gap. The standard way to decrease in single crochet is to pick up a loop in one stitch as well as the next. Yarn around the hook and draw through all three loops on the hook; these two stitches have now become one. In half double crochet, yarn around the hook and pick up a loop in one stitch (three loops are on the hook), yarn around the hook and pick up a loop in the next stitch (five loops are now on the hook), yarn around the hook and draw through all loops on the hook.

I've always found decreases in both these shorter stitches to be somewhat bulky, so I came up with a way to make them less so.

FOR A SINGLE CROCHET DECREASE. Pick up a loop from the first stitch, insert the hook into the second stitch and yarn around the hook. Draw the yarn through both the second stitch and the two loops on the hook. This almost feels like a slip stitch.

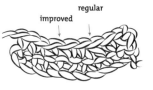

Increases in single crochet decrease

FOR HALF DOUBLE CROCHET DECREASE. Yarn around the hook and pick up a loop in one stitch, then yarn around the hook and insert the hook into the second stitch. Yarn around the hook and draw the yarn through both the second stitch and the four loops on the hook. This too feels like a slip stitch. These decreases are less bulky, and blend right in to the work so you won't even notice the decrease.

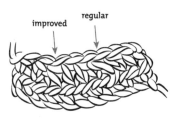

Increases in half double crochet decrease

● **TIP** KEEPING TRACK OF ROWS
Rather than having to constantly count rows from the beginning (especially troublesome in a long piece), mark off every ten or twenty rows. If you lose track of the rows, you'll only have to count from the last marker. If this piece will be seamed to another piece later, the marked rows will help you match up the pieces perfectly. Coilless safety pins, plastic diaper pins, or scrap pieces of yarn work well as markers.

● **TIP** EATING UP CROCHET

From time to time, instructions tell you to do something every so many rows. For instance, in a sleeve, you may have to increase a stitch at either end every fourth row six times, then every sixth row ten times. You keep track on paper but these tend to get lost. Here's the method my friend Claire Gregorcyk uses for counting. She sets out as many M&M™ candies as there are rows and eats one each time she comes to the end of a row. Once the candy is gone, she works the increase, decrease, or color change, and lines up another four or six candies (whatever number the pattern calls for). While not recommended for the diabetic, this trick does provide incentive to work faster. For those of us who are more health-conscious, peanuts or raisins work just as well. (Just make sure the dog and the kids are not around.) It's also a good idea to use a stitch marker to indicate the row where you've worked your increase or your decrease. That way, not only can you count more easily, you can see how many increases or decreases have been worked just by looking for the markers. I like to use one color marker for one set of instructions (like the every four rows, for example) and a different color for the other set.

Putting Down Your Work

I'm not talking about dissing that blanket
you're working on, but setting it aside. Unless
you crochet 24/7 (something I've been
known to try), you will eventually have to put
down your hook. You know what happens,
don't you? As you walk away, the yarn wraps
around your leg and your hard work starts
to unravel. To keep this from happening, place
a stopper on that last loop. A stitch marker
or coilless safety pin is best, but in a pinch a
paper clip will do just fine (I haven't had
much success with bobby pins, however).

**Then there's the hook. It always seems to
fall out, doesn't it? To keep it in place, insert
the hook in and out through the fabric and
wrap a rubber band or ponytail holder
around the top and bottom of the hook to
keep it in place.**

Securing the
crochet hook

Fixing Mistakes

• •

Missed a stitch? There's no need to panic.
Relax. Here are two ways to create a stitch
to replace one you skipped.

A MISSED STITCH ON THE PREVIOUS ROW.
Your row is 245 stitches across and you don't
want to have to rip out the row. If you are
working double crochet, you can fix this on the
current row. (This does not work for other
stitches.) Work to the stitch directly above the
skipped stitch. You will work an extra stitch
here. Go back into the stitch you just worked
in and yarn around the hook as usual. As soon
as you insert the hook into the stitch again and
pick up a loop, stop. Notice how the hook is at
the bottom of this row. Crochet into the
missing space of the row below by placing the
yarn around the hook, and then inserting the
hook into the missed stitch of the row below
and picking up a loop there. There are now
five loops on the hook. To complete the double
crochet stitch in the row below (yarn around
the hook and pull through two loops) twice.
Now go to the row that you're currently on to
finish the paused stitch: (yarn around the hook
and pull through two loops) twice again. It's
almost like a double treble crochet stitch. The
stitch is not perfect, but it works.

Fixing a missed stitch
in the previous row

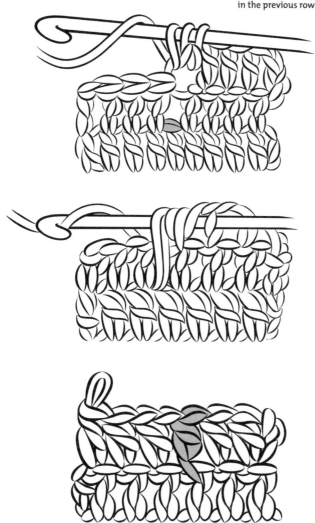

Fixing a missed stitch
several rows back

A MISSED STITCH SEVERAL ROWS BACK.
First, be sure to increase above the same
spot, even if it's several rows later, so the
stitch count remains the same. Although a
missed stitch is most glaring in a taller stitch
like double crochet and not as disastrous in
a shorter stitch like single crochet, this
fix works for all stitches. With the smoother
right side of the offending row facing you,
make a slip knot in a separate 12-inch
(30.5cm) strand of the same yarn and place
it on the hook. Work into the missed stitch
as you normally would. Fasten and end off
immediately. Finally, take out the slip knot
and weave both ends into the fabric. The gap
is now closed and no one will be the wiser.

Shortening Your Work

So you've finished your garment and find that it's too long. If this were an afghan or a scarf, you could just rip out at the top, but with a sweater, the neck has been shaped and the shoulder seams have been sewn. What's a crocheter to do? Easy, just take out from the bottom. It's not as hard as it sounds.

At the row just below the one you want to keep, clip the bottom of the last stitch of that row. Have a knitting needle (I like circulars, about two sizes smaller than the hook) or a tapestry needle threaded with smooth, contrasting cotton ready. Take a deep breath. Begin to pull out the clipped-stitch

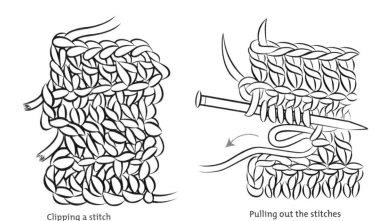

Clipping a stitch

Pulling out the stitches

row stitch by stitch. For every stitch above
the pulled-out stitch, place the needle
through the bottom of the newly released
stitch. There are two loops at the bottom of
these released stitches. Working through
both loops of each stitch at the underside
of these released stitches (and the one loop
of the beginning chain), slip stitch each
one of them to create a bottom chain to
finish off. If you are using a circular knitting
needle, you can do this from either end.
There, you're done.

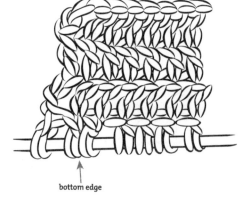

All the
stitches on a
needle

bottom edge

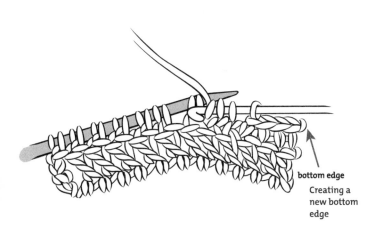

bottom edge

Creating a new bottom edge

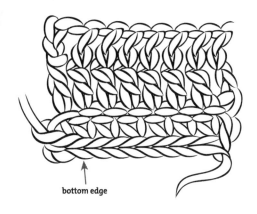

The new bottom edge

bottom edge

Major Surgery
• •

Even if you've messed things up big time—
say, by accidentally using the wrong dye lot
in the middle of your work, resulting in a
glaring difference in the yarns—there is an
alternative to ripping out all that hard work.
It's not difficult, but it is tedious. Begin as
if you were shortening a project (page 141)
by snipping the last offending row. The
bottoms of your stitches are now on, smooth
contrasting cotton or circular knitting
needle. Now you can rip out the mistake or
the wrong dye lot and rework up to the row
before the last offending one.

Make sure the wrong side (the one with
the bumps) of the top piece is facing you
since you will be working the right-side side
row right below it. As you work this last row,
after working each stitch, take the loop off
the hook and pull it through the correspon-
ding bottom two loops of the stitch above it.
To do this, use a crochet hook smaller than
the one you're working with and insert it
from left to right. Then place the loop back
onto the regular-sized hook to create
another stitch. Repeat for every stitch. (I told
you it's tedious, but would you rather rip?
I didn't think so.) After the very first
beginning chain, the loop goes under the

first stitch that you see, which is the last stitch of the row above.

If you're really ambitious, you can even repair fancier stitch patterns in this way. Even lace can be fixed by joining two or more stitch-bottoms together when pulling the dropped loop through. It's not for the faint of heart, though. If you're truly ambitious, you don't even have to substitute an entire row. Repair only the section with the mistake and carefully weave the many tail ends into the middle of the fabric later.

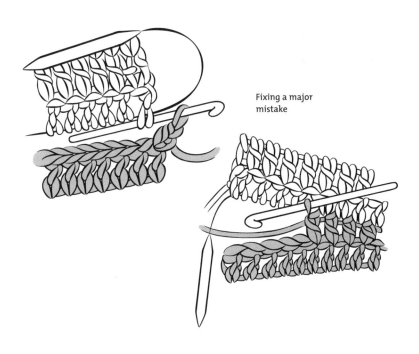

Fixing a major
mistake

In This Chapter

Finishing

Ready for that dreaded "f" word? (No, not *that* one.) Most of the crocheters I know hate the **finishing process.** "I want to crochet, not sew" is their cry. I like to quote my all-time favorite baseball hero, Yogi Berra. **It ain't over till it's over.**

Working Stitches Evenly Along Side Edges

The directions read, "Work 103 single crochet evenly along side edge," and you gulp. That edge is so long and daunting, how are you ever going to do it? Well I'm from the school of divide and conquer. Just break down that long edge into smaller chunks. To do that, fold the piece in half and mark the midpoint with a plastic locking stitch marker or a piece of scrap yarn. You now have two equal sections. Fold each section in half and mark the center again. You now have four equal sections. Fold each section in half yet again to create eight equal sections.

Now take the number of stitches along the edge and divide by the number of equal sections. For this example, that would be 103 ÷ 8 = 13, minus one (8 x 13 = 104, which is one more than you need). So between each marker, you'll work 13 single crochet, except in one section work only 12. The nice thing about this method is that, when you suffer from crochetus-interruptus, you'll only have to count from the last marker.

Another way to divide an edge into equal chunks is by measuring. If the edge is 21 inches (53.5cm) long, place a marker every 3 inches (7.5cm) to get seven equal chunks.

So 103 ÷ 7 = 15, minus 2. Since 7 x 15 = 105, that's 2 more than you need. Work 15 single crochet stitches in all but two sections. You'll work only 14 stitches in those two.

With either method, the phone can ring, someone can knock on the door, the kids can come in screaming, and the dog can bark at you, maybe all at once. You can still easily find where you left off without having to do all that counting.

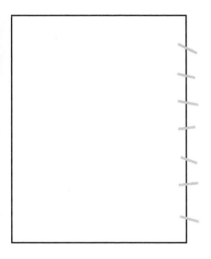

Evenly dividing the edge to be trimmed

Seaming

. . . .

Don't all groan at once. Done well, a seam can be a thing of beauty. There are several ways to sew things up, and you can even piece projects together without any sewing. The methods that follow can be used for side, top, and bottom seams, and curved seams like armholes and sleeve caps. Many crocheters like to pin or baste pieces together before seaming; if you've marked off every so many rows as you were crocheting (page 136), the markers will help you match equal portions of each piece.

When you start a foundation chain for a piece like a sweater that will require a seam, reel off some seaming yarn before you make the slip knot to eliminate an extra two ends to weave in later (one from the chain and one from the joined seaming yarn). One and one-half times the length of the seam is enough for mattress seaming. For example, if a sweater back has an underarm seam of 12 inches (30.5cm), reel off an extra 18 inches (45.5cm) for seaming. For back stitch seaming (which I personally seldom do), reel off three times the length of the seam, or 36 inches (91cm).

● **TIP** BREAD-TIE BOBBIN

Of course, you know what happens when
you add extra yarn to the chain, right?
You wind up working with the tail of the
seaming yarn rather than the yarn from the
skein. To avoid this, many crocheters roll
the long tail into a ball, which either gets all
knotted up or falls apart. To keep the seaming yarn separate, clean, and tidy while
you work, use the notched plastic bread tie
that comes with plastic-bagged bakery
products. (I've saved these for years.) Think
of them as free mini-bobbins, perfect
for wrapping seaming yarn. Just don't take
them off the bread on the supermarket
shelves—that's not nice.

Seaming yarn wound
on bread-tie bobbin

● **TIP** STARTING WITH A SLIP KNOT

If you did not reel off seaming yarn at the beginning of the project, you will have to attach new yarn now. To anchor the new yarn so it doesn't pop out as I'm sewing, I like to attach it with a slip knot. Make a slip knot in the tail yarn, insert the needle into the fabric, and then insert the needle through the slip knot before you tighten. Pulling through and tightening closes up the slip knot.

Starting with a
slip knot

● **TIP** ENDING WITH A FRENCH KNOT

I like to end my sewn seams with a French knot. To do this, wrap the yarn around the top of the needle a few times before inserting it into the last stitch. Pull to close tight.

A French knot

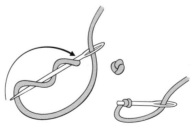

Whipstitch

The overcast or whipstitch is one of the easiest and most common seams, and it was probably one of the very first seams I made. Place the pieces with right sides facing each other and bring the needle from back to front (or vice versa) over and over again along the length of the seam. This is a relatively bulk-free seam, good for projects made of thicker yarns, and those made of textured novelty yarns where it is difficult to see individual stitches. It's a flexible seam, good for garments but not for items like purses, which are not meant to stretch.

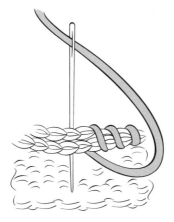

The whip-stitch seam

Back Stitch

Back stitching creates a strong, firm seam, great for shoulders. However, it is a bit bulky, so reserve it for worsted-weight yarns and thinner. Place the pieces with right sides facing each other. Think of back stitching as the bunny hop: Take two steps forward and one step back. That is, start from the right edge with the needle going from front to back through both fabrics; call this point A. Move to the left and insert the needle from back to front; call this point C. Insert the needle halfway between A and C from front to back; this is point B. Move to the left beyond C and insert the needle from back to front; this is point D. Now come from front to back through point C, and then back to front at point E. Continue this way: in through D and out through F, in through E and out through G, along the entire seam.

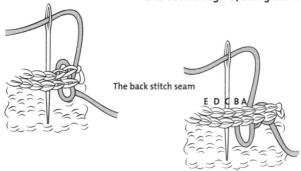

The back stitch seam

Slip Stitch

Many crocheters favor the slip stitch seam because it's like crocheting. Once again, have the right sides facing each other. Begin with a slip knot on the hook and * insert the hook through both fabrics from front to back, yarn around the hook and pull through everything—both fabrics as well as the loop on the hook. Repeat from the *. This is a sturdy, nonstretchy seam, good for coats and jackets and handbags. It is also quite bulky, so I would not recommend it for heavier yarns.

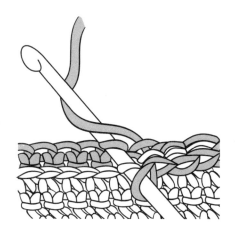

The slip
stitch seam

Single Crochet

Worked in a similar manner to the slip stitch
seam, the single crochet seam is crocheted,
not sewn. The difference is that you pull
up a loop after inserting the hook into both
fabrics, and then yarn around the hook
and pull through the two loops to complete a
single crochet. It's bulkier than slip stitch,
and slightly stretchier. It can also be used
decoratively on the outside of the piece.
If this is the look you want, place the wrong
sides facing each other and the right sides
to the outside. The beauty of the slip stitch
and the single crochet is that both are easily
taken out should you make a mistake.

The single
crochet seam

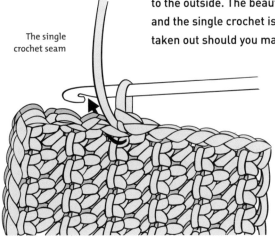

Mattress Stitch

Contrary to its name, mattress seaming does not require sewing in bed. I'm not certain where the name originated (perhaps it's because it lies flat?), but it is my all-time favorite seam. I find it the most invisible as well as one of the least bulky. And since you seam with the right sides facing you, you can always see what it looks like on the right side as you work. The only drawback is that it is very precise so there is little room for error. Each side must match exactly in the number of rows. Let me state again the importance of marking off every so many rows as you work (page 136).

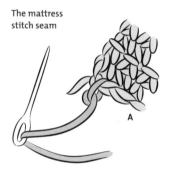

The mattress stitch seam

Let's start with the single crochet fabric first. Have the pieces abutting one another. I'll refer to the rows of one piece as A (1A, 2A, 3A), and the rows of the other piece as B (1B, 2B, 3B). Working with stripes allows you to clearly distinguish the rows.

If you've not reserved seaming yarn from the foundation chain, start with the slip knot join (page 152) on one side only, inserting the needle into the bottom end chain of A and tighten.

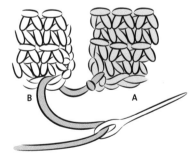

For either reserved seaming yarn or joined seaming yarn, go to the other piece and insert the needle from back to front of the bottom end chain of B.

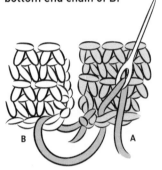

From here on, the directions are for both reserved seaming yarn and joined seaming yarn. Insert the needle from back to front of the end stitch of row 1A, and tighten.

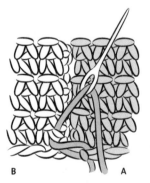

Now insert the needle from front to back of the bottom end chain of B and then from back to front of the end stitch of row 1B and tighten.

Insert the needle from front to back of the end stitch of row 1A and then from back to front of the end stitch of row 2A, and tighten.

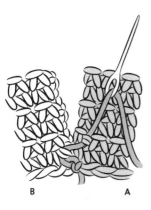

B   A

Insert the needle from front to back of the end stitch of row 1B and then from back to front of the end stitch of row 2B, and tighten.

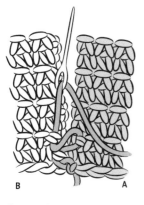

B   A

Insert the needle from front to back of the end stitch of row 2A and then from back to

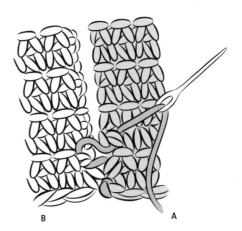

B   A

front of the end stitch of row 3A, and tighten.
Now insert the needle from front to back of
the end stitch of row 2B and then from back
to front of the end stitch of row 3B, and
tighten. Insert the needle from front to back
of the end stitch of row 3A and then from
back to front of the end stitch of row 4A, and
tighten. Now insert the needle from front to
back of the end stitch of row 3B and then
from back to front of the end stitch of row
4B, and tighten. Are you getting the idea? If
done correctly, the join is practically invisible (that's why tightening is important). Pull
on the seam itself every so often as you
work, but do not pull too tightly or the seam
will pucker. At the end, work a French knot
(page 152) with the needle going through
both thicknesses. Notice how the end

stitches of each side roll to the back. While this seam is not totally bulk-free, it's not bad. You can use mattress seaming for just about anything, but it's at its best for careful matching of patterns, such as stripes. When seaming taller stitches, such as half double crochet and double crochet, treat the top and bottom portions of these rows as two rows of single crochet and work into the end stitches themselves, not the space between stitches or you'd be constantly going into the same spot. In treble crochet, treat each stitch as three rows of single crochet.

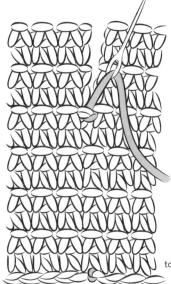

Pulling the pieces
together as you stitch

Joining As You Go

Believe it or not, it is possible to crochet a new piece and attach it to an existing one at the same time! Not only is there no seaming afterwards, but this join is also the most imperceptible and the least bulky of all. Of course, there are disadvantages as well. If you make a mistake, you'll have to rip out your work. The pieces have to match exactly, and they are joined to the right-hand side of the existing piece. That is, the new piece will wind up to the right of the old piece.

JOINING A NEW PIECE ON THE RIGHT. Starting with a single crochet fabric, place the existing piece with row 1 being the right side or smooth side facing. Think of the way row 1 was worked, you want this to be the side facing up.

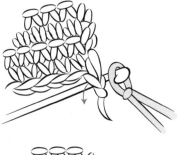

Joining as you go

To begin, make a slip knot with the new yarn and work a chain in the same direction. Insert the hook from front to back into the edge chain of the existing piece, place the slip knot on the hook, and draw the slip knot through to the front. Chain for the number of stitches needed for the new piece. See how they're joined at

Joining a new piece on the right

the bottom chain already?
For working purposes, we'll
call this the right side and
the other side will be
referred to as the wrong
side. Work a row of single crochet across
these new chains up to the last one. Pick up a
loop in this last chain, but before completing
this last stitch on the new piece, insert the
hook into the end stitch of row 1 on the old
piece first, then yarn around the hook and
draw through the end stitch as well as the
two loops on the hook to work a connecting
single crochet. This is a bit like my joining
of rounds when you close up gaps on the
last stitch of circular joins (page 131).

Normally, at this point in your
work, you would chain 1 and
turn. Here, instead of a chain 1,
slip stitch into the end stitch of
row 2 of the old piece as a substitute for the turning chain and
to connect the new piece to the existing
piece again. Then turn, bring the yarn to the
back, and single crochet across this wrong
side row. You have now completed two
rows of the new piece and connected each of
these two rows to the first two rows of
the old piece.

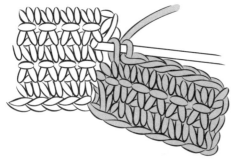

Work the next right-side row of single crochet or row 3, again to the last stitch. Pick up a loop in this last stitch but before completing this last stitch on the new piece, insert the hook into the end stitch of row 3 of the old piece first, then yarn around the hook and draw through the end stitch as well as the two loops on the hook to work another connecting single crochet.

Instead of working the turning chain-1, slip stitch into the end stitch of row 4 of the old piece to connect them again, turn, and bring the yarn to the back and single crochet across this wrong side row. You have now completed four rows of the new piece and connected each of these four rows to the first four rows of the old piece.

Continue in this manner, working a connecting single crochet at the end of the right-side rows and slip stitching into the next row before turning to complete the wrong side rows, matching row to row. This join looks so good and invisible that even when worked in a different color, there is total continuity of

fabric. I'd even do this instead of working
traditional intarsia (page 00). When creating
garments with this method, you can work
the left front of a cardigan first, then work
the back while joining to the left front, then
complete the right front of the cardigan
while joining to the back, and you'll never
have to work side seams.

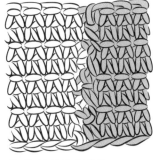

The finished seam after
joining as you go

Seaming as you go
cardigan

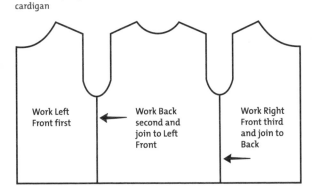

| Work Left Front first | Work Back second and join to Left Front | Work Right Front third and join to Back |

Seam from the back

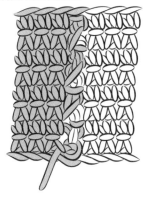

THE BACK OF THE SEAM. You might wonder
why the new piece is joined to the right of
the old piece. If you take a look at the back of
the seam, you will see ungainly joining threads.
Were you to work the connecting single
crochet on a wrong-side row and the slip

stitch on the row above it, you would see these ungainly joining threads on the right side of the work. Joining to the right avoids this.

JOINING A NEW PIECE ON THE LEFT.
Actually, I lied. You can join a new piece to the left-hand edge of an existing piece, but it's a little unorthodox. Work the chain of the new piece first, then drop the loop from the hook, insert the hook from back to front in the existing piece at the edge chain, and draw the dropped loop through to the back.

At this point, you would normally make an extra chain stitch to get to the height of the single crochet. Instead, loosen up the loop and drop it from the hook. Go into the end

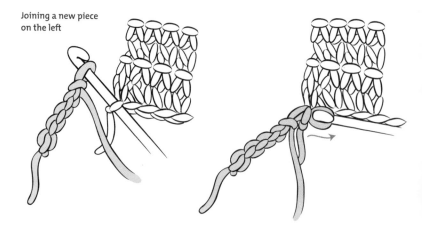

Joining a new piece on the left

single crochet of the old piece from front to back, place the dropped loop back onto the hook, and draw it through to the front of the fabric. With the right side still facing, single crochet across to complete the first row of the new piece, which is already joined to the first row of the old piece. Chain 1 and turn.

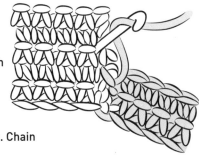

With the wrong side facing, single crochet to within the last stitch, pick up the loop in the last stitch, and stop. Bring the yarn to the wrong side of the work or the side facing you right now and insert the hook into the end stitch of row 2 of the old piece from back to front. Yarn around the hook and draw through the fabric as well as both loops on the hook to create a backwards-connecting single crochet. Switching the position of the yarn and the hook prevents the joining threads from showing up on the right side. The second row of the new piece is now connected to the second row of old piece, but backwards.

At this point, we need a turning chain, but this will also be backwards. With the yarn still in front of you, insert the hook from back to front of the end single crochet of

The finished seam

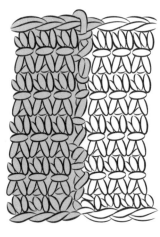

row 3, yarn around the hook and draw through for a backwards-connecting slip stitch. This connects the work to the third row of the old piece and gets you ready to work the third row of the new piece. Turn the work around and single crochet across the right side of the new piece.

With the wrong side facing, single crochet to within the last stitch, pick up the loop in the last stitch, and stop. Bring the yarn to the wrong side of the work or the side facing you right now and insert the hook into the end stitch of row 4 of the old piece from back to front. Yarn around the hook and draw through the fabric as well as both loops on the hook to create a backwards-connecting single crochet. Row 4 of the new piece is now connected to row 4 of the old piece, but backwards. With the yarn still in front of you, insert the hook from back to front of the end single crochet of row 5, yarn around the hook and draw through for a backwards-connecting slip stitch. Turn the work around and single crochet across the right side. Continue this way and the results are now clean on the right side. You can now join the front of a sweater to the back of the sweater in this manner at both ends, and not have to sew side seams.

CONNECTING WITH HALF DOUBLE CROCHET AND DOUBLE CROCHET. You can use the same method for half double crochet, but pull up on the loop a bit before working the connecting slip stitch to lengthen it for the height of a half double crochet. Insert the hook into the top of the end stitches when joining, rather than in the middle of the stitch. To join double crochet, there's just a slight difference. Just as for half double crochet, make the join at the top of the end stitches and not in the middle. Then, after working a joining double crochet, loosely chain first before working the connecting slip stitch to create the greater height of double crochet.

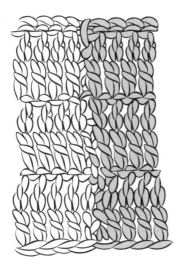

Seam as you go in double crochet

Blocking

• •

Blocking really should be done before
seaming, but I saved it for afterwards so as
not to scare you off. Full disclosure: I actually
block after seaming sometimes as well.
Blocking is way underrated; I'm rather
shocked at how few crocheters actually take
the time to block. Yes, it's an extra step but
think about what it can do for your crocheting.
The swatch on the left was steam blocked;
the one on the right was not.

Crochet, in its raw state, has a tendency to
curl, with the opposite corners curling
toward one another. This happens on the
back side of the work as well, and is true

Blocked
swatch

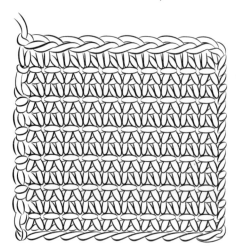

of all stitches. I've heard endless complaints about this curling, followed by requests for advice on how to fix or prevent it. Short of sticking the offending piece under a mattress for a week (and even that won't be a permanent fix), I highly recommend steam blocking, even for synthetics (more about this later).

Steam provides heat as well as moisture, and since it's the heat that sets a piece, it's important to use a really good steam iron. I actually have a floor steamer that looks like a vacuum cleaner hose connected to a water cooler. There's no metal to get hot so there's no chance of scorching. These steamers tend to be pricy, but they are so multipurpose that they're worth it.

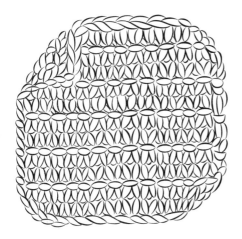

Swatch not blocked

My husband gets the wrinkles out of his shirt in the morning, a friend borrowed it to remove old wallpaper, and I use it for facials. Well worth the investment.

BLOCKING THE SWATCH FIRST. Try blocking, especially steaming, the swatch first. Steaming takes out any irregularities in your stitching, making it look better, but it can also relax the crocheting. You want to make sure that the results after steaming will still match your gauge. I often crochet slightly tighter than normal to make sure I get the gauge after steam blocking. When directions tell you to "block pieces to measurements," this is what they mean. After steaming, wool may lose a bit of its spring and loft as it softens. Steaming can add more slink to rayon or silk. To steam acrylic, use a good steam iron without ever touching the hot iron to the fabric, and move the iron around constantly, not hovering over any one spot for long. Allow the piece to dry thoroughly. I recommend that you do some testing on a few swatches, comparing steamed and nonsteamed pieces of the same swatches.

"KILLING A FABRIC." This industry term refers to very carefully pressing the fabric with a hot iron to permanently change its look, feel, drape, body, and texture forever. Whether this is a good or bad thing depends on the project and the individual crocheter. Many stitchers like the dressier sheen and drape on garments that have been pressed. A bonus is that once "killed," the stitches are set for life (I know, a bit of a contradiction here) and the fabric is stabilized. It will not grow any longer, or shrink any further. The gauge after killing should match the pattern's gauge. You can iron synthetics, too, but always place a pressing cloth over the project to avoid a sticky iron.

If you prefer more spring and loft in your fabric, wet block these projects. Let the project determine whether killing is appropriate or not, and always test it on the swatch first, especially when killing can radically alter your stitch gauge. Proceed cautiously since, as in real life, once killed, there's no resurrection.

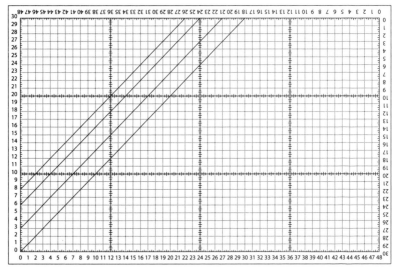

Blocking board
and T-pins

BLOCKING TOOLS. I like a good blocking board, and I have several. You can make one yourself using plywood and gingham fabric with one-inch squares. Lay some batting or an old blanket on the board, cover it with the fabric, and staple all around. Some crocheters have great success blocking on a foam board. It's become popular to use children's rubber jigsaw-puzzle flooring pieces for blocking, but if there's heat involved (as there is in steam blocking), I'd think twice about doing this and ending up with melted goo.

After washing and rinsing, lay the piece
on a towel to soak up the moisture. Use as
many towels as you need. If the piece is small
enough, you can use a salad spinner to
remove the water. Lay the damp piece to
measurement on the blocking board. Secure
the piece with pins every inch or so, or use
blocking wires, which I prefer. These
long flexible, stainless steel wires can be
inserted through all the edges to stretch the
pieces out to size. I find that using the wires
prevents the scalloping along the edges that
usually happens when using pins. For seamless garments in the round, you can use
the wires where the seams would be. If you
don't have a blocking board with a grid,
use a tape measure to lay the pieces to size,
then steam them, and let them dry.

The beauty of blocking before assembly is
that the edges lie flat and that makes seaming
easier. It's also easier to block the pieces
individually. After assembling, I steam the
seams for a polished look.

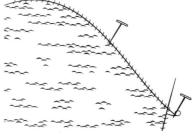

Blocking wires

Traditional end
stitch of a spiral

Ending Spirals

When working around in a circle without
turning, such as in a hat or a round bag or a
pillow, the directions often instruct you not
to join the rounds. In essence, you go around
and around in a spiral. This is usually done
in a short stitch, such as single crochet, though
it's found in half double crochet as well.

Notice how at the end of the piece, the last
stitch is high and the next one over is low.
How ugly is that? Most of the time, you slip
stitch into the last stitch to minimize the
height difference, and then fasten off. In half
double crochet, you'd single crochet in the
second to last stitch, then slip stitch in the last
stitch. Even this leaves a bit of a blip.

● **TIP** SPIRAL DUPLICATE STITCH

My solution to this blip is to use a duplicate chain stitch. Work the last single crochet and clip the yarn, leaving a 6-inch (15cm) tail. Then pull on that last loop on the hook until the tail pops out, and thread it onto a yarn needle. Notice where the tail came out.

Spiral with the end tail pulled out

At the base of the tail is the chain over the last stitch. You will use the tail yarn to create what is known as a duplicate stitch. As the name implies, this stitch creates a false chain, joining this last stitch to the rest of the fabric, invisibly and seamlessly. Skip the next stitch, since the false chain will substitute for a stitch over this one. Insert

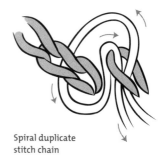

Spiral duplicate stitch chain

Spiral joined with a
duplicate stitch

the needle underneath both legs of the
chain over the following stitch, and pull
the yarn through. Insert the needle into the
chain the tail popped out of, and put
the remaining tail behind the work to be
woven in, pulling just tightly enough on the
tail so that the duplicate stitch chain mimics
the other size of the other chains.

Other than seeing the tail, you can't tell the
beginning from the end anymore. Is this a
smooth finish or what?

Joining Tops of Stitches to Each Other

• •

When joining the shoulders of a sweater, pillow tops, the bottom of a handbag, or even motifs like granny squares, the tops of stitches are joined to the tops of other stitches. Of course, you can use any seaming method (pages 150–161), but if I can avoid sewing, I will. Just as we can join a new piece to the old along the side edges in the join-as-you-go technique (page 162), you can join tops of stitches.

ON A RIGHT-SIDE ROW. Start with the wrong sides of the pieces touching; the right sides are on the outside. You will work this joining row when you have one row to go on the new piece and you are ready to work a right-side row. After completing the first stitch, drop the loop from the hook. Insert the hook from back to front of the first stitch of the old piece, place the loop back on the hook, and draw through.

Joining the tops of stitches: the first stitch

After completing each subsequent stitch, drop the loop from the hook and pull it through the next accompanying stitch from front to back again as follows: Insert the

Joining tops of
stitches: the row

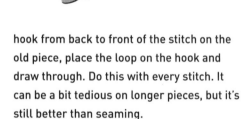

hook from back to front of the stitch on the old piece, place the loop on the hook and draw through. Do this with every stitch. It can be a bit tedious on longer pieces, but it's still better than seaming.

ON A WRONG-SIDE ROW. To work a wrong-side row on the new piece, place the pieces so the right sides are touching and the wrong sides are facing out. After completing each stitch, draw the dropped loop from back to front by inserting the hook from front to back.

Drop-shoulder Sleeve Seam

When you sew the sleeves to the body in a drop-shouldered garment, the stitches at the top of the sleeves are being joined to the rows of the body and the stitch gauge is not the same as the row gauge. In single crochet, the stitches are short and wide. In double crochet, the stitches are tall and skinny. So when you sew sleeve stitches to body rows in single crochet, you will skip a row occasionally. When you sew sleeve stitches to body rows in double crochet, you will do the opposite. You will sew about two stitches to each row. The problem is that the stitches and rows are not always so perfectly matched.

To make the seaming easier you can single crochet the same number of stitches down the armhole as there are stitches at the top of the sleeves. Join the shoulder seam first. Count the number of stitches at the top of the sleeve. Mark off the armhole and divide evenly (page 148), then single crochet that number of stitches along the marked armhole. There are now exactly the same number of stitches along the rows of the armhole and each one of these stitches can now be joined to each stitch of the sleeve. No more counting.

Why single crochet and not any other stitch? These are "joiner" stitches and you want them to be as imperceptible as possible. Their sole purpose is to give you a seaming guide.

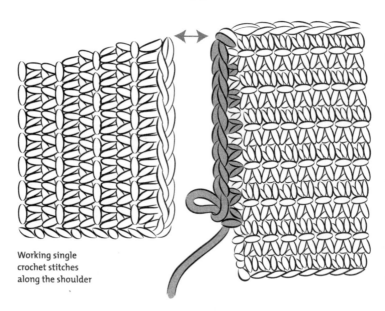

Working single crochet stitches along the shoulder

Spacing Buttons Evenly
· ·

When it's time to make the button and
buttonhole bands on a cardigan, the instructions may say something confounding like
"place seven ⁵/₈-inch (16mm) buttons evenly
spaced along the button band, with the top
button ¹/₄ inch (6mm) from the top edge and
the bottom button 2 ¹/₂ inches (6.5cm) from
the bottom edge." How frustrating. But I've
got an idea.

Take a piece of white elastic, about ¹/₂- to
1-inch (13mm-2.5cm) wide and about a foot
long. Lay it down flat and draw big dots with
a magic marker every inch. These 1-inch
(2.5cm) markings represent the number of
buttons you'll be using, but the markings
will not stay 1 inch (2.5cm) apart for long.
Choose the number of dots to represent the
number of buttons called for in the pattern.
Fasten down the top of the elastic ¹/₄ inch
(6mm) from the top edge of the jacket or
cardigan front and pull on the elastic until the
bottom dot is 2 ¹/₂ inches (6.5cm) from the
bottom edge. Use straight pins to mark the
dot placement on the sweater—you can
replace them later with a marker or a piece
of scrap yarn.

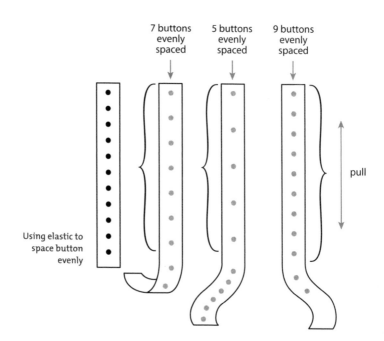

7 buttons evenly spaced

5 buttons evenly spaced

9 buttons evenly spaced

pull

Using elastic to space button evenly

You can also purchase an expandable trivetlike device called the Simflex™ to evenly space things for you, but the elastic is handy, and inexpensive, and can be used for other projects like placing flowers evenly spaced across a pillow.

Making Buttonholes
· ·

Now that you've evenly spaced the buttons,
you need to make buttonholes. Buttonholes
are almost always worked in single crochet.
Other stitches are too tall and the space
between them can be mistaken for an
unintentional buttonhole. Convention says
to single crochet up to the buttonhole area,
chain a certain amount, say, two, three,
or four stitches, and skip the same number
of stitches, then continue to single crochet.
On the next row, you single crochet into each
of the chains.

I've always been dissatisfied with this
method because the stitches on either side
of the buttonhole have loose strands that
can catch the button as it is passed through.
And the buttonhole is often too big.

Even a one-stitch buttonhole is made
larger because of the height of the single
crochet on either side of it. At a typical

Making a
traditional
buttonhole

Loose strands
in a traditional
buttonhole

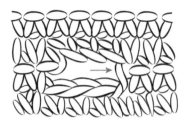

gauge of four stitches per inch, the buttonhole is more than $1/4$ inch (6mm). A
two-stitch would be $1/2$ inch (12mm). Most
buttons for garments are $3/8$ inch (10mm)
or $1/2$ inch (13mm) or $5/8$ inch (16mm).

● TIP A TIGHT BUTTONHOLE

Here's how to make a gap-free buttonhole.
Work up to the place where you want the
buttonhole. Working into the same place as
the last single crochet, begin a foundationless single crochet (page 95). Work as many
foundationless single crochet as there are
skipped stitches.

After working about three foundationless
single crochets, you will skip the next
three single crochet. Before working into
the next single crochet, insert the hook into
the chain of the last foundationless single
crochet worked, then insert the hook
into the stitch. Yarn around the hook and
draw the loop through first the stitch, then

the foundationless chain portion, yarn around the hook and complete the single crochet. Continue to the place for the next buttonhole and repeat.

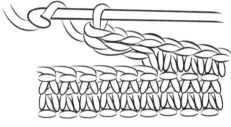

Making a tight buttonhole

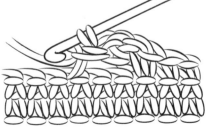

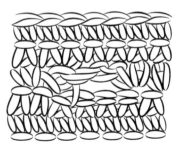

Sewing on Buttons

Sewing on buttons is another one of my least favorite things to do. There are two kinds of buttons: those with holes and those with shanks. I love shanks, and there are several reasons they're the only kind I will use. With a button with holes, not only is the thread visible, the button winds up being too close to the fabric, and as a result, when you button the button band over it, the button band can dimple in like a pincushion.

A traditional sewn shank

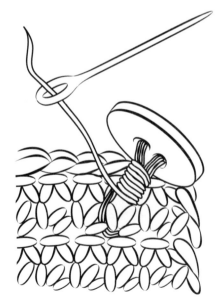

The traditional fix for this is to place a toothpick or coin below the button before you start sewing, creating a space between the button and the band. After attaching the button, you make a shank by wrapping more thread around the thread used to sew on the button. Too much of a big knotted mess for me.

Crocheting Buttons On

I have not sewn on a button in over fifteen years. I crochet my buttons on. Here are two ways to do it.

USING DENTAL FLOSS. For the first method, you need a shank button and a 4-inch (10cm) piece of dental floss; the waxed type is better. You will use the floss to thread a stitch

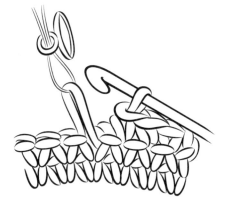

Using dental floss

A button on
the loop

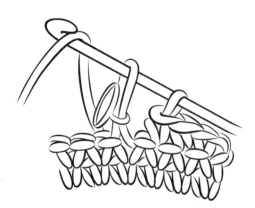

through the shank hole of the button. Work
up to where you want the button to be, pick
up the loop in the stitch, place the loop onto
the dental floss, and then put both ends of
the floss together and draw them through
the hole of the shank, pulling until the loop
goes through the shank hole. Place the loop
back on the hook, take out the floss, make
sure the button is facing the right way, and
complete the single crochet.

USING A CROCHET HOOK. For the second
method, you need a shank button and a steel
crochet hook small enough to go through
the hole in the shank. Insert the small crochet
hook through the shank hole of the button
and set it aside. Single crochet to where you
want the button to be, pick up the loop in the
stitch, and place this loop on the small crochet

hook. Pull the loop through the shank hole and place the loop back onto the regular hook, make sure the button is facing the right way, and complete the single crochet.

The hook method is faster, but the dental floss method may be more convenient as most of us have dental floss around. Take a close look at the crocheted-on button and you'll see that there are two strands of yarn holding the button firmly in place.

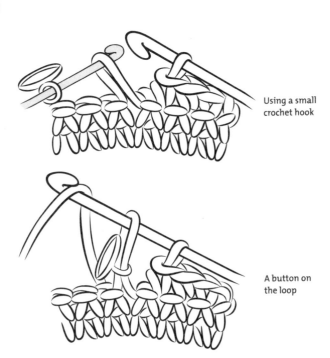

Using a small crochet hook

A button on the loop

If you plan to crochet on your buttons, keep the following in mind:

- No sharp shanks. The edges will saw at the yarn and eventually break your work.
- No delicate fibers. Some yarns, like angora, almost fall apart when you tug at them.
- No heavy buttons. Heavy metal or solid glass will pull too much on the one stitch.
- No loose gauges. The button will pull out the stitch and distort the work.
- Beware the directional button. That heart may be on its side depending on how it sits on the shank. The letter U can become a C.
- Use buttons that are washable.
  Lastly, make sure you won't change your mind. If you want to replace the buttons, you'll have to rip out your work.

You can apply beads to your work in the same manner. This is a real timesaver because you don't have to string the beads onto the yarn ahead of time. What a boon! In fact, I devote a couple of chapters to this method in my book, *Knit and Crochet with Beads*. Check it out.

Crocheted Buttons

· ·

When you want buttons to match your project perfectly, your best bet is what's known as a self-button. These are buttons crocheted from the same yarn used to make your project. You may find similar versions, but I've perfected the directions so no sewing is involved. (See? I told you I try to avoid having to sew.)

Mark the rounds of your crocheted buttons with a piece of contrasting yarn (do not join the rounds). Use the smallest hook possible to get a sturdy button. Make a slip knot with the tail (page 00) leaving about a 4-6 inch (10-15cm) tail. Keep the tail in front of the work at all times.

Row 1: (The wrong side is always facing you, the backside is the right side): Single crochet six or eight stitches into the slip-knot ring.

Keep the yarn tail in front as you work

Row 2: Work two single crochet in each single crochet around to double the number of stitches (twelve if you had six, sixteen if you had eight).

Row 3: Single crochet in each single crochet around. The work will curl toward you, forming a button or mushroom cap shape.

Row 4: Single crochet in *every other* single crochet around, decreasing the number of

Pulling both tails to close the button

The finished button

stitches back to the original six or eight. If you plan to stuff the button with a bit of yarn or fiber filling, do so now, still keeping the yarn tail in front.

Row 5: Slip stitch in *every other* single crochet around, reducing the number of stitches to half (either three or four).

End off yarn, leaving a 4-6 inch (10-15cm) tail and pull this tail through the last loop to fasten off, pull tightly.

The beauty of this button is that you now have two tails. If you pull on the original tail from the beginning slip knot, it closes up the hole completely. To attach the button, insert each of the tails in either side of a stitch in the fabric, and tie both ends together in a square knot at the back of your garment or project. No need to sew. Don't you just love it?

Weaving in Ends

The key to weaving in ends is to take many
U-turns in your path. A straight line, like
the running stitch, will come out easily. Try
to change directions as often as possible,
up and down, left and right. Take a look at the
proposed directions that the yarn end can
take in this swatch.

The tool of choice for most of us is the
darning needle. I adore the bent-tipped
Chibi brand. The bent tip really allows you to
dig deep into the little nooks and crannies.

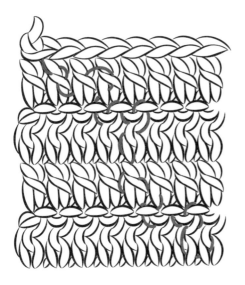

A path for weaving
in a yarn tail

● **TIP** WORKING WITH SHORT ENDS

Most of my ends are not longer than about 2 inches (5cm). I just heard a big thud. It's true. The reason I can get away with this is the reversal of directions that I just talked about. Yet how I can maneuver after threading the needle? The trick is to not to thread the needle first. Insert an empty darning needle near where the end is, weave it in and out through the fabric in a diagonal line, then thread the yarn end into the needle and draw it through the fabric.

Threading the short end onto the needle *after* weaving the needle through the fabric

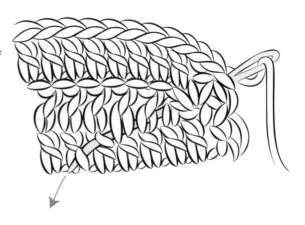

Using a Latch Hook

When holding a yarn needle to weave in ends, I can use two or three fingers at most. I like to get a better grip; I'd rather hold something firmly in my hand with a knife hold for better leverage. Using a smaller crochet hook can snag the yarn. Luckily, I also happen to be machine knitter and machine knitters have really cool tools. One of these is the latch hook, which looks like the kind used for latch-hook rugs, but smaller. Mine is double-ended; the smaller end is meant for thinner yarns and the larger end for thicker yarns. I find it easier to handle than a yarn needle.

When the latch is open, it's shaped like a hook; when the latch is closed, there's

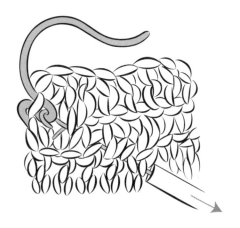

Securing a yarn end
using a latch hook

no open hook to catch or snag the fabric. To use a latch hook, start at the end where you want the yarn to end up, then work back toward the yarn tail. You have to move the stitches behind the hook in order to close the latch over the yarn end and then pull the tail through.

You can keep the ends of really slippery fibers like rayon or silk from unraveling by dabbing on a bit of Fray Check. Try this out on your swatch to make sure it won't cause the yarn to bleed or form a too-hard ball or bead.

The yarn tail woven in

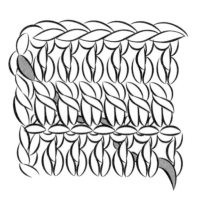

● **TIP** BRUSHING MOHAIR OR EYELASH YARN

Just as some fabrics look better with the nap raised, some yarns, like mohair and eyelash and sometimes even alpaca, angora, and brushed acrylic, can use a little fluffing up from time to time. Crocheted fabric that's meant to be furry will eventually mat down with wear and washing. A touch-up with a brush can infuse new life into these fabrics. If your stitches are uneven or there are some mistakes you want to hide, brushing is great for that, too. You can use a soft metal-bristled pet brush from a pet supply store—I'm sure the pooch won't mind if you borrow it from time to time.

The Lowdown
from Lily

USE THE BEST MATERIALS, hooks and yarns best suited for each other and the ones you're most comfortable with, because **crocheting should be fun!**

ALWAYS MAKE A SWATCH. Do I have to say it again? Always make a swatch. Better to use up half a ball of yarn and half an hour of my time than waste a dozen balls of yarn and a month of my time.

EMBRACE YOUR MISTAKES. We crocheters are so hard on ourselves as we strive for perfection. Don't point out your mistakes, the ones no one else can see; **be kind to yourself.** My motto has always been: If a one-eyed man on a galloping horse can't see it, fuhgedaboutit! (in my best Brooklynese).

THINK AHEAD. Reel off seaming yarn (if needed) ahead of time for fewer ends to weave in later. Use clothespins to anchor your foundation chain before joining in a circle to keep the stitches straight. Know how many yards of yarn go into a row of your work so you don't run out partway through. Taking the time to take a breath before you begin can be **the best time-saving tactic.**

PAY ATTENTION TO DETAILS. Evenly space picked-up stitches as well as buttonholes and buttons. Mattress seam precisely for invisible seams, with stripes lined up perfectly. Work the beginning and end of a spiral circle so the join is **smooth and continuous.**

PROBLEM SOLVE. The things that bother you usually have a solution. Problem solving means figuring out what's wrong (analysis), then breaking down components that get in the way of desired results (evaluation). In **explaining the logic** of how some of my tips have come about, I encourage you to come up with **your own ideas and "a-ha" moments.**

Crochet Abbreviations

approx	approximately
beg	begin/beginning
bet	between
ch(s)	chain(s)
ch sp	chain space
CC	contrasting color
cont	continue/continuing
dc	double crochet
dec	decrease/decreasing
foll	following
hdc	half double crochet
hk	hook
inc	increase/increasing
lp(s)	loop(s)
MC	main color
pat or patt	pattern
pm	place marker
prev	previous
rem	remain/remaining
rep	repeat
rnd(s)	round(s)
RS	right side
sc	single crochet
sh	shell
sk	skip
sl st	slip stitch
st(s)	stitch(es)
tog	together
tr	treble crochet
WS	wrong side
yo	yarn over hook

Resources

Clover Needlecraft, Inc.
13438 Alondrea Blvd.
Cerritos, CA 90703
(562) 282-0200
http://www.clover-usa.com
Chibi darning needles, stitch markers, light-up crochet hooks, bamboo crochet hooks, other notions.

Coats and Clark
P.O. Box 12229
Greenville, SC 29612-0229
(800) 648-1479
http://www.coatsandclark.com
Susan Bates crochet tools.

Fiber Fantasy Knitting Products, Ltd.
4876 Butler Road
Glyndon, MD 21071
(410) 517-1020
http://www.woolstock.com
Blockers kit and fold-away blocking board.

Fiber Trends
P.O. Box 7266
East Wenatchee, WA 98802
(509) 884-8631
http://www.fibertrends.com
Needle-felting supplies.

Four Paws
50 Wireless Blvd.
Hauppauge, NY 11788
(631) 434-1100
http://www.fourpaws.com
Pet brushes.

Handler Textile Corp.
60 Metro Way Dept #G
Secaucus, NJ 07094
(201) 272-2000
http://www.goliath.ecnext.com
Space Board gridded blocking board.

Knitcraft
215 North Main
Independence, MO 64050
(816) 461-1248
http://www.knitcraft.com
Machine knitting latch hook.

Prym Consumer USA Inc.
950 Brisack Road
Spartanburg, SC 29303-4709
(864) 576-5050
http://www.dritz.com/askus/faq/faq_04.php
Fray Check seam sealant.

Wm. Wright Co.
85 South Street
P. O. Box 398
West Warren, MA 01092
(877) 597-4448
http://www.wrights.com
Boye crochet hooks.

Bibliography

Brown, Nancy. *The Crocheter's Companion.* Loveland, CO:
Interweave Press, 2002.

Chin, Lily. *Couture Crochet Workshop.* Loveland, CO: Interweave Press, 2007.

Chin, Lily. *Knit and Crochet with Beads.* Loveland, CO: Interweave Press, 2004.

Kooler, Donna. *Encyclopedia of Crochet.* Little Rock, AR: Leisure Arts, 2002.

Manthey, Karen and Brittain, Susan. *Crocheting for Dummies.* Indianapolis, IN:
Wiley Publishing, Inc., 2004.

Acknowledgments

I want to thank Rosie Ng, who's been ever so patient with me all
these years. Of course, there's Melissa Bonaventure, not to mention
Erica Smith and Betty Wong. Not many people can say that
their attorney is also a good friend and fellow knitter/crocheter, but
Margo Lynn Hablutzel is all that to me, and more. I'm grateful to
Linda Hetzer for listening well and pushing gently and filling in nicely.
Most of all, thanks and praise go to tech editor Karen Manthey,
who's seen me through three books now. Lastly, I would not be able
to do this without the love and support of my long-suffering husband,
Cliff. Oh, my computer and scanner and digital camera have been
totally indispensable.

Index